The History of the Bible: The Making of the New Testament Canon

Bart D. Ehrman, Ph.D.

THE
GREAT
COURSES

PUBLISHED BY:

THE GREAT COURSES
Corporate Headquarters
4840 Westfields Boulevard, Suite 500
Chantilly, Virginia 20151-2299
Phone: 1-800-832-2412
Fax: 703-378-3819
www.thegreatcourses.com

Bart D. Ehrman, Ph.D.

Professor of Religious Studies
The University of North Carolina at Chapel Hill

Professor Bart D. Ehrman is the James A. Gray Professor and Chair of the Department of Religious Studies at The University of North Carolina at Chapel Hill. With degrees from Wheaton College (B.A.) and Princeton Theological Seminary (M.Div. and Ph.D., magna cum laude), he taught at Rutgers for four years before moving to UNC in 1988. During his tenure at UNC, he has garnered numerous awards and prizes, including the Students' Undergraduate Teaching Award (1993), the Ruth and Philip Hettleman Prize for Artistic and Scholarly Achievement (1994), the Bowman and Gordon Gray Award for Excellence in Teaching (1998), and the James A. Gray Chair in Biblical Studies (2003).

With a focus on early Christianity in its Greco-Roman environment and a special expertise in the textual criticism of the New Testament, Professor Ehrman has published dozens of book reviews and more than 20 scholarly articles for academic journals. He has authored or edited 16 books, including *Misquoting Jesus: The Story Behind Who Changed the Bible and Why* (San Francisco: HarperSanFrancisco, 2005); *Truth and Fiction in the Da Vinci Code* (New York: Oxford University Press, 2004); *Lost Christianities: The Battles for Scripture and the Faiths We Never Knew* (New York: Oxford University Press, 2003); *Jesus: Apocalyptic Prophet of the New Millennium* (Oxford University Press, 1999); *The New Testament: A Historical Introduction to the Early Christian Writings* (Oxford, 1997; 3rd ed., 2004); and *The Orthodox Corruption of Scripture* (Oxford, 1993). He is currently at work on a new commentary on several non-canonical Gospels for the *Hermeneia Commentary* series, published by Fortress Press.

Professor Ehrman is a popular lecturer, giving numerous talks each year for such groups as the Carolina Speakers Bureau, the UNC Program for the Humanities, the Biblical Archaeology Society, and select universities across the nation. He has served as the president of the Society of Biblical Literature, Southeast Region; book review editor of the *Journal of Biblical Literature*; editor of the Scholar's Press Monograph Series *The New Testament in the Greek Fathers*; and co-editor of the E. J. Brill series *New Testament Tools and Studies*. Among his administrative responsibilities, he has served on the executive committee of the Southeast Council for the Study of Religion and has chaired the New Testament textual criticism section of the Society of Biblical Religion, as well as serving as Director of Graduate Studies and Chair of the Department of Religious Studies at UNC.

Table of Contents

The History of the Bible:
The Making of the New Testament Canon

The History of the Bible:
The Making of the New Testament Canon

Scope:

There can be no question that the New Testament is the most important book—or collection of books—in the history of Western civilization; it is by far the "bestseller" of all time, since the invention of printing. But many people today do not know a lot about the New Testament, including such basic facts as what books it contains, when they were written, by whom, when, and for what purpose; how the books were copied and transmitted down through the ages; and when and why they came to be collected together into a canon of Scripture.

This course is designed to answer these basic questions about the New Testament. We will begin with an overview of what the New Testament contains in broad terms. We will then move to a consideration of the earliest writings of the New Testament, the letters of the apostle Paul. En route, we will consider some basic information about how books were actually written in the ancient world, before there were word processors, photocopy machines, typewriters, or movable type. What writing materials were used? How were books published? How did they get circulated?

We will then consider Paul's letters themselves, asking why they were written, what crucial issues they address, and what message they convey. In a subsequent lecture, we will consider the circumstance that there were other letters in circulation in early Christianity that *claimed* to be written by Paul but probably weren't. This will lead us to consider the widespread phenomenon of *pseudepigraphy* (forgeries in the name of a famous person), both in the ancient world at large and in the early Christian movement itself.

From there, we will move to a consideration of the Gospels. These books differ from the Epistles in that they are not merely compositions of a single author but embody traditions about Jesus that had been in circulation by word of mouth for decades before the authors produced their accounts. We will begin our examination by asking how the oral circulation of these traditions affected them—were some of the stories in the Gospels modified from how they originally happened? Were some of them actually made up?

We will then look at the earliest Gospels we have—which are those of the New Testament, Matthew, Mark, Luke, and John—to see who their actual authors were and to understand the messages they tried to convey in their narrations of the birth, life, death, and resurrection of Jesus. As we will see, these four were not the only gospel records that we have; in our next lecture, we will examine some of the other Gospels, those that did not make it into the New Testament.

From there, we will move to a broader consideration of how these various books—Epistles, Gospels, and other writings—have come down to us today. We will look at how books were published and distributed in the ancient world and consider, in particular, how they were copied in an age in which the only way to make a new copy of a book was to reproduce it by hand, one word at a time. How did the copying processes affect the words of the text? Were the words ever changed, so that we don't know what the author originally wrote?

We will continue our investigation by asking why these various books were so widely circulated, noticing on the way that Christianity was unusual in the ancient world for placing such a heavy emphasis on literary texts as authorities for faith and practice. One problem, however, is that different Christian communities had different understandings of the faith—and all of them had "authoritative" books (allegedly by apostles) that promoted their own understandings of the faith.

The wide range of surviving "apostolic" literature is one of the factors that drove Christians to decide on a specific *canon* of Scripture, that is, one collection of books that could be accepted as providing the authoritative basis for the faith. But even agreeing on which books to include did not solve all the problems, because different readers can interpret the same text in different ways. Thus, Christians also devised rules for interpreting these sacred books.

We will conclude the course by looking at the question of when the canon came to be finalized, establishing for all time the contours of the Christian Scriptures, the New Testament as it has come down to us today.

Lecture One
The New Testament—An Overview

Scope: This course will deal with some of the most fundamental questions about the New Testament Scriptures: How did we get the 27 books of the New Testament? When and how were the books written? For what purpose? How were they circulated and transmitted? When were they collected into a canon of Scripture?

We begin, in this opening lecture, by dealing with some of the basic facts about the New Testament: which books it contains, when they were written, in what language, and by whom. This will be a good "refresher" for those who are already familiar with the Christian Scriptures and vital information for those coming to these books for the first time.

Outline

I. Despite its vast importance and popularity, the New Testament remains an "unknown book" to many highly educated people today.

   A. It is rarely read, let alone studied, outside of church settings (contrast other bestselling books!).

   B. As a result, it is accepted as authoritative much more widely than it is known.

   C. I realize this anew every year in my introductory New Testament course that I teach at UNC, when I begin the class with a pop quiz on basic information about the New Testament—with students who say they believe in the Bible but clearly don't know what is in it.

II. There can be little doubt that the New Testament is the most important book in the history of Western civilization.

   A. It lies at the foundation of the largest and culturally most significant religion in the West.

   B. It is the "book of faith" for millions of Christians still today.

    C. It continues to be not only the all-time bestseller but also an important cultural artifact in popular culture, as can be seen in such movies as *The Passion of Christ* and such novels as *The Da Vinci Code.*

III. This set of lectures is meant to provide an introduction to the New Testament for people who recognize its historical and cultural importance but who have not yet had a chance to get to know where it came from, what it contains, and how it was transmitted down to us today.

    A. Our focus will be on *historical* information about the New Testament; the course does not presuppose either faith or skepticism.

    B. The course is designed for anyone interested in knowing more about the most important book in the history of our culture.

    C. It will address some of the key questions people have about the New Testament.
        1. What kinds of books does it contain?
        2. When, how, and why were these books written?
        3. What do these different books teach?
        4. How did these books get collected into a *canon* of Scripture?
        5. How did they get transmitted down through the ages until today?

IV. We can start in this lecture with some of the most basic information about the New Testament.

    A. The New Testament contains 27 separate books, written by 14 or 15 early Christian authors for other Christian communities and individuals.

    B. The books are our earliest surviving Christian writings of any kind, written in the 1st century A.D.

    C. All the books were originally written in Greek.
        1. Greek was the *lingua franca* of the early Roman Empire.
        2. It was not the language of Jesus or his earliest followers (who all spoke Aramaic) but was the language of most of the Christians of the second generation, when these books started to appear.

D. The books of the New Testament are arranged in four groups, according to genre.

    1. The New Testament begins with the Gospels: four accounts of the life, ministry, death, and resurrection of Jesus.

    2. It continues with the book of Acts, a historical account of the life of the Christian Church and its missionary efforts after Jesus' resurrection.

    3. It then contains 21 Epistles, actual letters written by Christian leaders, most prominently the apostle Paul, to Christian communities and individuals, dealing with problems of faith and living.

    4. It ends with an apocalyptic vision of the end of the world as we know it, the Revelation of John.

E. There were other Christian books written at about the same time as these that did not come to be included in the New Testament.

    1. One of our questions will be why these 27 books came to be privileged as sacred Scripture when the others, ultimately, did not.

    2. Another question will be how the books that did become the New Testament came to be transmitted through the ages, until the invention of the printing press could make them more widely available. (As we will see, we don't have the originals of any of the books of the New Testament, only later copies.)

V. Before getting to these questions, we should examine more closely the basic contents of the New Testament books.

A. The Gospels are our earliest accounts of the life, death, and resurrection of Jesus.

    1. Scholars usually differentiate between the *synoptic* Gospels, on the one hand, and the Gospel of John, on the other.

    2. The synoptics (Matthew, Mark, and Luke) tell many of the same stories, often in the same words.

    3. John has its own set of stories and a completely different style of presentation.

    4. All four of these are to be seen as *gospels*—that is, proclamations of "good news"—rather than as objective biographies by research historians of the day.

B. The book of Acts, as well, is driven not by purely historical interests but by a powerful theological agenda: to show that God was at work in the spread of the Christian mission.

    1. It traces the spread of Christianity from its inauspicious beginnings just after the death of Jesus to its auspicious arrival, after the missionary work of Paul, in the capital of the empire, Rome itself.

    2. One of the questions scholars have brought to its account concerns its historical accuracy in light of its clear theological agenda.

C. The Epistles of the New Testament are usually divided into those written by Paul, on the one hand, and the *catholic* (or universal) Epistles, written by a range of authors, on the other.

    1. Among the 13 letters that go under Paul's name, 7 are generally acknowledged as having come from his hand.

    2. For the most part (with one exception), these deal with problems that had emerged in the churches that Paul had established as a Christian missionary in what are now Greece and Turkey.

    3. Six other letters claim Paul as their author, but scholars have long harbored doubts that they were actually written by him. These so-called *Deutero-Pauline Epistles* appear to have been composed by later followers of Paul to deal with problems that had emerged in their own day.

    4. There are 8 other letters in the New Testament, written by various authors to deal with a variety of problems. Here again, some of the letters (such as 2 Peter) may not actually have been written by their alleged authors. We will deal with the issue of Christian *pseudepigraphy* (the writing of books under a false name) in the course of our lectures.

D. The Revelation of John is the one apocalypse of the New Testament. We will want to explore how apocalyptic literature worked in early Christianity (and Judaism) in order to see how this book—rather than providing a blueprint for the future, as is often claimed—is best situated in its own historical context to provide a message of hope for those who were experiencing turmoil as followers of Christ.

VI. In sum, the New Testament is a much-varied and intriguing collection of books, with different authors, different genres, different audiences, different agendas, and different teachings. In this course, we will examine both the contents of these writings and the questions of how they were gathered into one canon of Scripture and handed down through antiquity until today.

Essential Reading:

Raymond Brown, *An Introduction to the New Testament*, chapter 1.

Bart D. Ehrman, *A Brief Introduction to the New Testament*, chapter 1.

Supplementary Reading:

Bart D. Ehrman, *Lost Christianities: The Battles for Scripture and the Faiths We Never Knew.*

Harry Gamble, *The New Testament Canon: Its Making and Meaning.*

Questions to Consider:

1. In your opinion, why does the New Testament continue to be such a culturally and religiously important book for people today?

2. What do you imagine would be different about our culture if all references to the New Testament were somehow removed from it?

Lecture One—Transcript
The New Testament—An Overview

I'd like to welcome you to this course on *The History of the Bible: The Making of the New Testament Canon.* The New Testament is one of those books that's more widely recognized as important than it is read or understood. I saw this in a graphic way this past year in my undergraduate course on the New Testament, teaching at the University of North Carolina at Chapel Hill. This is one of these large undergraduate classes with 400 students in it. I teach in this large auditorium and have an army of graduate students who are my teaching assistants who do all the grading for me. At the beginning of this class this past semester, I decided to take a bit of a survey of my students, and so I asked them the following question: How many of you, I asked, would agree with the proposition that the Bible is the inspired word of God? Vroom, the entire room raises its hand. I said, "All right, how many of you in here have read *The Da Vinci Code?*" Vroom, the entire room raises its hand. I said, "All right, how many of you in here have read the entire Bible from cover to cover?" The response was scattered hands throughout the room. So I said, "I don't quite understand this. I'm not telling you that I think God wrote the Bible, you're telling me that you think God wrote the Bible. I can see why you might want to read a book by Dan Brown, but if God wrote a book, wouldn't you want to see what he had to say?" I'm afraid the situation isn't limited to my class of college undergraduates.

The New Testament is appreciated and respected far more than it's known, and that's not just true among religious people who consider themselves Christian, for the New Testament is a huge cultural artifact in our day. It's an important book whether or not a person happens to believe in it, because it's an important cultural artifact. This can be seen in a number of ways. For example, it's seen in recent movies that have appeared such as Mel Gibson's movie, *The Passion of the Christ,* which at the box office, among movies rated R, was the highest grossing film of all time. Some people thought it was gross for other reasons. The film is based on Jesus' last hours, allegedly as reported in the Gospels. It's impossible to evaluate the film, however, unless you know something about the Gospels.

The New Testament, as an enormous cultural artifact, can be seen in other ways as well; for example, in the novel, *The Da Vinci Code,* which is predicated on an idea that the Gospels of the New Testament in fact present a cover up; that in point of fact, contrary to what you find in the Gospels, the historical Jesus was actually married to Mary Magdalene, and they had a child who was the beginning of the Merovingian Dynasty in France. How does one evaluate claims such as that without the knowledge of the New Testament? In fact, it's impossible. But most people don't have any knowledge of the New Testament, and that's the raison d'être of this course.

This set of lectures is designed to provide an introduction to the New Testament for people who recognize its historical or cultural importance or who have religious commitments to it, but who have not yet had a chance to get know where it came from, what it contains, and how it was transmitted down to us today. The focus in this course about the New Testament will be historical, rather than theological. This course does not either presuppose faith or deny faith. It's based neither on faith nor skepticism.

Sometimes it's hard for my undergraduates to understand the difference between an historical approach to the New Testament and a theological approach; so, I try to explain it to them in terms they can understand. The historian can differentiate between the theology of Gandhi, on the one hand, and Martin Luther King, Jr., on the other. The historian can tell you what each person thought, but the historian cannot tell you which person was right about their theological beliefs. The historian can tell you what happened during the Reformation as the Protestants fought the Catholics, and can tell you what the theological issues involved were. But, the historian cannot tell you which side was on the side of God; the historian doesn't have any particular access to God, only to events that happened in this world. The historian can tell you that Jesus died on the cross and can tell you the circumstances surrounding his death, but the historian, as an historian, cannot tell you that Jesus' death was for the sins of the world; that's a theological judgment to be made by theologians, something that the historian, as an historian, cannot say.

This class, then—that we'll be covering in 12 lectures—deals with the New Testament, but it is not taught from a theological perspective of faith. It's simply taught from the perspective of history. It's designed for anyone who's interested in knowing more about the most important book in the history of our culture, the New Testament.

The class will address several key questions that people may have about the New Testament. What kind of books does the New Testament contain? When, how, and why were these books written? What do these different books teach? How did these books get collected into a canon of scripture, a collection of books that believers call the canon of scripture? And how did these various books come to get transmitted down through the ages, until today?

We can start, in this lecture, with some of the most basic information about the New Testament. The New Testament contains 27 separate books, which were written by 14 or 15 Christian authors for Christian communities and individuals. So, the New Testament isn't just one book; in fact, it's 27 different books. These 27 books are our earliest surviving Christian writings of any kind. They were all written in the first century A.D.

Now, I want to make sure we're all on the same chronological timeline. The modern calendar divides itself, roughly on the basis of Jesus' birth. As it turns out, the calendar is somewhat off. Jesus, evidently, was born sometime around the year 4 B.C., which means Jesus was born four years before Christ, which is a bit confusing, but it's because when the calendar was made in the Middle Ages, the monk Dionysius Exiguus, who made up the calendar, made a mistake about when Jesus was born. In any event, the era is divided with the birth of Jesus, B.C., before Christ; A.D., year of our Lord, *Anno Domini,* meaning the time after Jesus' birth. Jesus was born, then, 4 B.C. He probably was executed around the year A.D. 30. The Gospels and the other books of the New Testament were written after that— 30, 40, 50 years after that. Almost all of the books in the New Testament, though, are written within the first century A.D.

These books were originally written in Greek. When I teach this large undergraduate class, one of the questions that I initially ask them, just to see how much they know about the New Testament, is, "In what language were the books of the New Testament written?" Remarkably, some, of course, think it was written in English. Apart from those, of the people who do know it was written in an ancient language, many of them think it was written in Hebrew, which is wrong. The Old Testament, the Hebrew Bible, the Jewish scriptures, were written in Hebrew, but all of the books of the New Testament, were originally written in Greek. This is because Greek was the lingua franca of the early Roman Empire. Since the conquest of Alexander the Great, some three centuries earlier. when Alexander the Great spread Greek culture throughout the entire Mediterranean, it became common for the elite throughout the Mediterranean to speak Greek. So, if you wanted to communicate broadly in the Roman world, you didn't use Latin, the language of Rome, you used Greek, the language of international culture and commerce. Much as today, English is spoken throughout much of the world, in those days Greek was spoken throughout much of the world.

So, the New Testament contains 27 books from the first century written by 14 or 15 different authors, written in the Greek language. I should point out that Greek was not the language spoken by Jesus and his followers. Jesus and his followers, who were all Jews living in Palestine, spoke the local language, which was Aramaic. Aramaic is a language that's closely related to Hebrew; it's different from Hebrew, but it's closely related to Hebrew, and that was the language of Jesus. So that when you read the New Testament Gospels, you read in them English. The English is a translation of the Greek original of the Gospels, but the Gospels written in Greek are, in fact, translations of Jesus' sayings, which were in Aramaic. By the time they come to you, you're getting them third-hand.

The books of the New Testament, the 27 books of the New Testament, are arranged typically in four different groups, according to their various genres. There are four major genres within the New Testament. The New Testament begins with the Gospels, four accounts of the life, ministry, death, and resurrection of Jesus: Matthew, Mark, Luke, and John. These give us the beginning of Christianity in the life, death, and resurrection of Jesus. Second, the New Testament contains the book of Acts, which is a historical account of the life of the Christian church and its missionary efforts after Jesus' resurrection. The book of Acts continues the story of what happened to Jesus' followers after he had died and been raised from the dead. The third section of the New Testament consists of 21 Epistles. These are actual letters written by Christian leaders—most prominently, the apostle Paul—to Christian communities and individuals dealing with problems of faith and living. With the Gospels we have the beginning of Christianity, with the book of Acts we have the spread of Christianity after his death, and with the Epistles we have the beliefs and ethics of Christianity. Finally, the New Testament ends with an apocalyptic vision of the end of the world as we know it, the Book of Revelation, sometimes called the Apocalypse of John. This book, then, gives us the climax of Christianity. These, then, are the four main genres of the New Testament.

I should point out that there were other Christian books written at about the same time as these books that are in the New Testament, other Christian books that did not come to be included among the Christian scriptures. We have access to other Gospels, other Acts, other Epistles, and other Apocalypses. There are other gospels, for example, allegedly written by the apostle, Peter, or the disciple Philip, even a Gospel allegedly written by Mary Magdalene. We have other Acts besides the Acts of the Apostle in the New Testament, for example, the Acts of John and the Acts of Paul, accounts of the missionary exploits of some of the apostles after Jesus' death. We have other Epistles that did not make it into the New Testament, some of them claiming to be written by Paul; for example, a set of letters that were exchanged between Paul and the Roman philosopher Seneca, allegedly. We have other Apocalypses that didn't make it into the New Testament, most famously one called the Apocalypse of Peter, which is the first surviving account we have of a guided tour of Heaven and Hell. Jesus takes Peter on a tour of the realms of the blessed and the damned, a very interesting book that almost made it into the New Testament. One of our questions in this course will be why the 27 books that made it into the New Testaments came to be privileged as sacred scripture, whereas these other books, also allegedly written by apostles, did not come to be seen as scripture.

Another question that we'll have will be how the books that did come to be the New Testament came to be transmitted down through the ages, until the invention of the printing press could make them more widely available. Before the printing press was invented, the only way for a book to be transmitted and reproduced was by having it copied by hand. Well, what happens when you copy a book out by hand, one word, one letter, at a time? Unfortunately, when you do that, you often make mistakes. Mistakes were made frequently in these copies and we don't have the original copies any longer. What we have are copies that were made hundreds of years after the originals. So how do we know what the originals actually said? That's one of the questions we'll be dealing with in the course.

Before getting to these various questions, we should examine more closely the basic contents of the New Testament books according to the four major groupings that I've already indicated. First, let's talk about the Gospels, our earliest accounts of the life, death, and resurrection of Jesus. These four books—Matthew, Mark, Luke, and John—are usually divided into two groups by scholars. The first group are the synoptic Gospels of Matthew, Mark, and Luke. The synoptic Gospels are called synoptic from a Latin word, which means "seen together," because the synoptic Gospels of Matthew, Mark, and Luke tell many of the same stories, often in the same words, frequently following the same order. You can put Matthew, Mark, and Luke in parallel columns next to each other and can compare their stories with one another and can see, then, that they're telling the same story. So, they're synoptic because they can be seen together.

These three Gospels—Matthew, Mark, and Luke—tell the same basic story about Jesus. In two of them, Matthew and Luke, he's born of a virgin in

Bethlehem. The gospel of Mark is different, because it begins with Jesus as an adult. But from there on, the stories have very similar outlines. Jesus gets baptized by John the Baptist; he goes into the wilderness to be tempted by the Devil; he comes back; and he begins proclaiming the coming of the Kingdom of God. He teaches the crowds in parables; he performs many miracles, including casting out demons. Halfway through his ministry, he goes up onto a mountain in the presence of three of his disciples and he is transfigured before them, the Mount of Transfiguration. He predicts that he needs to go to Jerusalem to be betrayed and denied, and to be put on trial and then executed, but that then he will rise from the dead. He then makes a trip to Jerusalem the last week of his life. He overthrows the tables of the money-changers in the temple and causes a ruckus in the temple, which leads to the anger of the high priest, who decides to have him turned over to the Roman authorities. He is turned over to Pontius Pilate, who condemns him to death by crucifixion. Jesus then is crucified, and on the third day, he's raised from the dead.

You find the same basic story in Matthew, Mark, and Luke. Sometimes, within the basic story, you have exact accounts in Matthew, Mark, and Luke. There are verbatim agreements: you'll have the same story, word-for-word agreement. The only explanation as to why you can have this word-for-word agreement, in the opinion of most scholars, is that one of these Gospels is being used as a source for the other two. In other words, there must be copying going on.

I sometimes have difficulty convincing my students that if you have three accounts of the same event that are in the same words, somebody has to be copying somebody else. The way I try to convince these 19- and 20-year-olds of this is, I do this little exercise where I come into class a couple of minutes late to make sure everybody's there; I fiddle around in front of the class; I turn on the overhead projector; I put down my briefcase; I roll up my sleeves; and I do a few things. And then I ask everybody in the class to take out a pen and paper and to write down everything they've seen me do in the last three minutes. The students, all 400 of them, write down what they've just seen me do. Then I take four volunteers. I collect four papers and I say, "Now, I want you all to do a synoptic comparison. I'm going to read what each of these sources has to say, and I want to know whether you have a sentence that is exactly like someone else's." Then I do a comparison of these four accounts in which they describe what they've seen me do, and in all of my years of doing this—15, 16 years of doing this—I've never had anybody with two sentences exactly the same.

So then I ask my students, "What would you think would happen if I took up two of these pieces of paper and I had two paragraphs that were verbatim, the same, exactly alike?" They say, "Well, somebody copied off from someone else." Exactly, somebody copied from someone else. I say, "Now imagine I didn't do that today. Suppose I waited 30 or 40 years, and, instead of asking you to write down what happened that day in class, I asked friends of yours that you had told about what had happened in class, and I got two accounts and they were exactly the same? What would you assume had happened?" There's always some wise guy in the back row that raises his hand and says, "It's a miracle." Right.

Well, those are the two options, actually: it's either a miracle, or else somebody's copying somebody else. By the way, if it's a miracle, if what's happened is that this is divinely inspired, and that's why you have so many word-for-word similarities, you have a very big problem, because you have not only similarities between the three Gospels, you have vast differences between them as well. There are discrepancies between the Gospels. If you explain the similarities on the basis of miracle, then you have trouble explaining the discrepancies. We'll be talking about the discrepancies in a later lecture, but they do exist. People don't notice the discrepancies among the Gospels because of the way people read the Gospels. The way people read the Gospels is they read Matthew, it's about the life and death of Jesus; then they read Mark, and it sounds a lot like Matthew sounded; then they read Luke, and that sounds a lot like Matthew and Mark sounded. When you read them this way, what I would call reading them vertically, one at a time, they all sound very much alike, so you don't notice the differences. The way to notice the differences among the Gospels is to read them not vertically, but to read them horizontally, where you read one story in Matthew, then you read the same story in Mark, and the same story in Luke. You'll have word-for-word agreements, but you'll also have discrepancies and you'll notice these discrepancies. Some of these discrepancies, in fact, are very hard to reconcile with one another.

Those are three Gospel accounts—Matthew, Mark, and Luke—called the synoptic Gospels that have so many agreements because they have the same sources. What scholars think today is that Mark was the first Gospel written, and that Matthew and Luke both had access to Mark, and used Mark as one of their sources. Matthew and Luke had other sources available to them as well.

The Gospel of John is different from Matthew, Mark, and Luke. The Gospel of John does not contain most of the stories found in the synoptic Gospels.

For example, in John there's no account of Jesus actually being baptized. There's no account of his birth either. There's no account of him going to the wilderness to be tempted by the Devil. Jesus never tells a parable in the Gospel of John. Jesus never casts out a demon in the Gospel of John. Jesus does not go up to the Mount of Transfiguration in the Gospel of John. Jesus does not have his last supper, in which he gives out the bread and the wine and says, "This is my body, this is my blood," in the Gospel of John. Jesus is not put on trial before the Jewish Sanhedrin in the Gospel of John. There are wide-ranging differences where John doesn't have the same stories as the synoptics. John has a different set of stories; it has a different set of miracles, including the first miracle in the Gospel of John where Jesus turns the water into wine, always the favorite of my students at Chapel Hill when it comes to the miracle stories, the turning of water into wine. John has many dialogues between Jesus and someone else that are found only in John. For example, there is Jesus' discussion with Nicodemus in chapter 3, or with the Samaritan women in chapter 4. Many of Jesus' sayings are found in John, only in John. John, then, stands out as a unique Gospel; some people have called it a maverick Gospel.

All four of the Gospels are best understood as Gospels. The term "Gospel" means "good news"; it comes from the Old English word, *gōdspel*—"good news." These books do not claim to be objective histories; they claim to be proclamations of good news. In other words, these books are not historically accurate accounts of things that Jesus said and did that you would have been able to capture on videotape if you had been there. These are books that are proclaiming information about Jesus that is meant to provide information needed for salvation. These books are the good news of Jesus' life, death, and resurrection.

Second in the New Testament is the book of Acts. The book of Acts is also driven not by historical interests, pure and simple, but also by a theological agenda, just as the Gospels are driven by a theological agenda. The book of Acts attempts to portray the spread of Christianity as the work of God. It traces the spread of Christianity from its inauspicious beginnings just after the death of Jesus, to its auspicious arrival after the missionary work of the apostle Paul in the capital city of Rome, the center of the empire itself. The point of the book of Acts is that Christianity has spread. It has spread from being just a Jewish sect to being a worldwide religion; and it has spread geographically from its beginnings in Jerusalem to the capital city of the empire itself, the city of Rome.

The Epistles of the New Testament are usually divided into two groups. As I pointed out earlier, there are 21 Epistles in the New Testament. The two groups are Epistles that are written by Paul, or allegedly written by Paul, on the one hand, and the so-called Catholic Epistles, or universal Epistles, or general Epistles, on the other hand, which are written by a range of authors. Of the 21 Epistles in the New Testament, 13 of them go under Paul's name; so, over half of the Epistles in the New Testament are allegedly written by Paul. But as we'll see in a later lecture, scholars have come to think that some of these Pauline letters, in fact, are not written by Paul. At least six of the 13 letters under Paul's name are disputed by scholars as to whether Paul actually wrote them or not. Many scholars think that six of these letters were written by later followers of Paul, who were using Paul's name in order to write an Epistle.

The letters that Paul himself wrote, especially the seven undisputed letters, are all written to Paul's churches. They're written in order to deal with problems that had arisen in the churches that Paul had established as a Christian missionary. Particularly in the areas that we now call Greece and Turkey—those were the two regions that Paul was most active in as a missionary. He established churches in those areas and his modus operandi was that he would go to a city and establish a church there by converting people to faith in Christ. Then, after he had taught them some things, he would go to the next city and convert people there and establish a church there. Then, he'd go to another city. Invariably, he would hear about problems in the churches he left behind. The letters are meant to address those problems. The letters are meant to address the problems in Paul's churches, problems that people are having about what to believe, and problems about how they are to behave as Christians. Those are the letters of Paul.

Six other letters, then, are letters that scholars have called Deutero-Pauline letters because they appear not to be by Paul himself, but to have been composed by followers of Paul to deal with the problems that emerged in their own day.

The other eight letters of the New Testament, the Catholic, or universal, or general Epistles, are written by a variety of authors to deal with various problems in the church. Here, again, I should say that some of these letters, for example, 2 Peter, may not actually have been written by their alleged authors. We'll be dealing with this issue of Christian pseudepigraphy, of writing books under a false name, in the course of our lectures.

Finally, there's the Book of Revelation. Revelation is the one Apocalypse of the New Testament. In our study of the apocalypse, we'll want to see how this book, rather than providing a blueprint for our own future, as it's often claimed, is, in fact, best interpreted as being a book written for its own historical context, to provide a message of hope for those who are experiencing turmoil as followers of Christ. The Book of Revelation continues to be read by people as if it's a blueprint for our own future; that it's telling what's going to happen in the years to come. One of the most popular books in modern times, apart from *The Da Vinci Code*, is a series of books called the *Left Behind* series that many of you will have known about. The *Left Behind* series uses the Book of Revelation to describe what's going to happen in our future. But is this a correct interpretation of what will happen in our future, or, in fact, is this a misinterpretation of the point of the Book of Revelation? The *Left Behind* series, by the way, isn't the first phenomenon of its kind. In the 1970s, the best-selling book in the English language was a book called *The Late Great Planet Earth* by Hal Lindsey. It sold more copies than any other book in English, except for the Bible. This was a book that predicted, in graphic detail, how the end of the world was going to come by 1988. Obviously, it didn't happen, and so what came as a result? Well, the author wrote another book. The Book of Revelation, I'll be maintaining, is best understood in its own historical context, rather than as a book that is intending to give a blueprint for our own future.

To sum it up, the New Testament is a much varied and intriguing collection of books with different authors, different genres, different audiences, different agendas, and different teachings. In this course, we will be examining both the contents of these writings and the questions of how they were gathered into one canon of scripture and handed down through antiquity until today.

Lecture Two
Paul—Our Earliest Christian Author

Scope: To the surprise of many readers, the *earliest* books of the New Testament were not the Gospels but the Epistles of Paul, which were produced in the 50s A.D., some 20–25 years after Jesus' death (and about 20–25 years before the Gospels). These Epistles are actual pieces of correspondence: Paul was writing letters to churches he founded in order to deal with difficulties that had arisen. Because he couldn't visit all these churches at once, his letters served as a substitute for his apostolic presence.

In this lecture, we will consider what it meant to write a letter in the ancient world. How were letters produced, published, and disseminated? What kind of writing materials (e.g., papyrus) were used? What physical form did letters take? As we will see, these questions lead to some interesting issues that affect how we understand Paul's Epistles and the other writings of the New Testament.

Outline

I.   In our last lecture, we looked at the books of the New Testament in broad outline; in this lecture, we consider in a little more depth the earliest writings of the collection: the letters of the apostle Paul.

   A. Many people mistakenly assume that the Gospels were the first books of the New Testament to have been written.

   B. In fact, the letters of Paul were written at least 15 or 20 years before our earliest Gospel and are the earliest surviving writings from any Christian author.

   C. These are letters, for the most part, that Paul wrote to churches that he had established in Asia Minor, Macedonia, and Achaia—modern Turkey and Greece.

   D. In them, we learn not only about the difficulties that the Christian Church was facing in the early years of its existence but also about the life and teachings of Paul himself, who was arguably the most important figure in the history of Christianity after Jesus.

E. In this lecture, we will briefly explore the life and teachings of Paul and begin to examine the letters that he wrote, looking specifically at what it meant to write a letter in the ancient world.

II. Some have argued that without the apostle Paul, Christianity would have been radically different or, possibly, that it never would have come into existence as a major world religion.

    A. Our sources for knowing about Paul's life are regrettably sparse, including the book of Acts (in which he figures prominently) and occasional references to his own past letters.

    B. Paul started out not as a follower of Jesus but as an avid Pharisaic Jew who persecuted the church.

        1. Early Christians maintained that Jesus was the Jewish messiah who had died for the sins of the world.

        2. Most Jews did not anticipate a messiah, but some Jews thought the messiah would be a warrior who would drive out the Roman occupiers; others saw the messiah as a heavenly being; and others expected him to be a great priest.

        3. No one expected that the messiah would be a crucified criminal.

        4. The first Christians came to see Jesus as the messiah from their reading of passages in the Jewish scriptures that talk about one of God's righteous ones suffering for the sins of others (cf. Isaiah 53; Psalm 22).

        5. These passages don't explicitly refer to the messiah, but Christians claimed they did.

        6. Jews saw Jesus simply as a crucified criminal; to call him the messiah was blasphemous. This was the reason Paul persecuted the Christians.

    C. But in one of the great turnarounds in all history, Paul converted from being a persecutor of the Christian Church to being its greatest advocate and missionary.

        1. It appears that he had a visionary experience of Christ in the course of his own persecution of Christians.

        2. This changed everything for him: He no longer saw Jesus as one who was cursed by God (in his crucifixion) but one who fulfilled God's own purposes.

3. He reasoned that Jesus' death must have had a divine purpose and concluded that Jesus' death was the way God deals with sin—it brought a right relationship with God.

4. Paul probably continued to keep Jewish Law, but came to believe that following the Law could not put a person in right standing before God; only Christ's death could do that.

5. Paul also came to believe that, Jesus' resurrection signified that the end of time was near. Paul believed, as did many Jews, that the end of time and the Last Judgment were near.

6. He believed Jesus was raised from the dead as the "first fruit," meaning that the celebration of the "harvest" (the end of time) had begun; Jesus would return to Earth in glory and this would happen in Paul's own lifetime.

7. Once convinced of this, Paul began proclaiming his new faith in Jesus as the one whose death could restore people to a right standing before God.

8. With the help of others, he began establishing churches in non-Jewish "pagan" (that is, Gentile polytheist) lands.

9. His modus operandi involved moving to an urban setting, converting pagans to believe in the one true God and Jesus as his son, forming them into worshiping communities, and then moving on to the next city to start anew.

10. When he would hear of problems in the churches he had left behind, he would write letters to them in order to deal with the problems.

III. Writing letters in the ancient world was, in many ways, similar to writing letters today, but there were some key differences.

A. Letters were often dictated, because very few people could write. (Paul, at least, knew how to pen a few words and sign his name.)

B. They could be written either on papyrus—a writing surface made out of the papyrus reed—or on wax tablets.

C. They were not mailed but hand-delivered by someone traveling to where the recipient lived.

D. They were often destroyed after they were read; if there was a reason to keep the letter, it might be copied by hand and circulated more broadly.

E. Paul's letters appear to have been "read" by the churches he sent them to, which meant, necessarily, that they were read aloud in community settings.

IV. Paul's letters were, by and large, written to deal with problems of his churches, involving both how to live and what to believe.

    A. One clear example of a letter that is concerned with Christian lifestyle is Paul's first letter to the Corinthians.

        1. The Corinthians were experiencing numerous problems in their congregations: divisions in the church, instances of flagrant sexual immorality, questions about ethical dilemmas (such as whether it was right to eat meat that had been sacrificed to a pagan deity), and issues involving their worship services.

        2. Paul deals with each of these questions one by one, giving his pastoral advice.

        3. It is clear that the letter he writes stands in for his apostolic presence, because he could not be everywhere at once, but numerous churches depended on his insights and advice.

    B. An example of a letter that is concerned with proper Christian belief is Paul's letter to the Galatians.

        1. Here, the concerns are less ethical than doctrinal: Should Gentile Christians accept and follow the Jewish Law to be true members of God's chosen people?

        2. Whereas some Christian missionaries who had arrived in the Galatian community urged its members to follow the Law, Paul saw this as a real perversion of the truth of the Gospel.

        3. He urges Gentile converts not to try to attain God's favor by becoming Jewish.

V. By reading Paul's letters, we can get a sense of the kinds of problems the earliest Christian communities were experiencing, as well as a sense of the teachings and theology of Paul himself, which will be the subject of our next lecture.

Essential Reading:

Bart D. Ehrman, *A Brief Introduction to the New Testament*, chapters 12–15.

Calvin Roetzel, *The Letters of Paul: Conversations in Context*.

Supplementary Reading:

Gerald Hawthorne and Ralph Martin, *Dictionary of Paul and His Letters*.
Leander Keck, *Paul and His Letters*.

Questions to Consider:

1. Can you think of problems that might be created for interpreting Paul's teachings by the circumstance that the only way we have access to them is through personal letters he wrote?

2. Can you imagine ways Christianity would have been different if Paul had never converted to the faith?

Lecture Two—Transcript
Paul—Our Earliest Christian Author

In our last lecture, we looked at the books of the New Testament in broad outline. In this lecture, we consider in a little more depth the earliest writings of the collection, the letters of the apostle Paul. Many people mistakenly assume that the Gospels were the first books of the New Testament to have been written. They are, after all, the first books in the New Testament, and so the natural assumption is that, when you start reading the New Testament with Matthew, Mark, Luke, and John, you are reading the earliest writings of the collection. But that's not the case. Even though the Gospels occur earlier in the New Testament, they were not the first books to have been written. The letters of Paul were written 15 or 20 years before our earliest Gospel, Mark. This makes Paul's writing the earliest surviving writings that we have from any Christian author. The books in the New Testament are our earliest Christian books, and among those, the writings of Paul are the earliest of them all; so that, from the letters of Paul, we have the earliest Christian writings that survive.

The letters of Paul are, for the most part, books, epistles that Paul wrote to churches that he had established in Asia Minor, Macedonia, and Achaia, which were territories that are today known as Turkey and Greece, where Paul was most active as a missionary. As I pointed out in the previous lecture, in these letters of Paul, we learn not only about the difficulties that the Christian Church was facing in the early years of its existence, but we also learn about the life and teachings of Paul himself, who was arguably the most important figure in the history of Christianity, after Jesus.

A number of years ago, maybe 20 years ago now, there a survey was taken of college professors in a variety of fields—history, political science, philosophy, classics—in which they asked these professors who, in their opinion, was the most important person in the history of Western civilization. Now, if I were to ask that question of my class at Chapel Hill, the answer would come back, Jesus was the most important person in the history of Western civilization; and, in fact, I think a case could be made that Jesus was the most important person. As it turns out, though, in this particular survey, Jesus came in tied for fifth. He tied with the apostle Paul for fifth place. The most important person in the survey, to the surprise of my students, was Alexander the Great. The logic was that Alexander the Great was the one who spread Greek culture throughout the Mediterranean world. Without Greek culture, our form of civilization wouldn't exist. The

Romans eventually conquered basically the same region that Alexander the Great had conquered. They continued to perpetuate Greek customs and culture and religion and language, so that this became the culture of the Mediterranean world that was inherited after the Roman Empire, down into the Middle Ages, down to today; so that on this logic, Alexander the Great was the most significant figure in the history of Western civilization because without him, Jesus would not have been able to make the impact that he did.

In any event, in this survey it's interesting that Paul and Jesus tied for fifth. Why would they tie? In the opinion of the scholars who were being surveyed, they tied because without Paul, the religion that Jesus promoted would not have become what we call Christianity. According to this opinion, Jesus was a Jewish prophet and teacher who didn't start out to found a new religion. They said that Jesus preached about the God of the Jews, and he taught about the Hebrew Bible, and the law of Moses, and how people could best follow the law. They viewed it that Jesus was a Jew promoting a form of Judaism. Paul, however, changed the religion of Jesus, so that it was no longer the religion of Jesus, but it was the religion about Jesus.

The opinion is that the apostle Paul transformed the teachings of Jesus to the teachings about Jesus' death and resurrection. That what mattered for Paul was that Jesus died on the cross and had been raised from the dead and that this brought salvation. It's interesting that when you read through Paul's letters, Paul rarely talks about Jesus' own ministry. Paul rarely quotes any words of Jesus. Paul almost never mentions anything that Jesus did during his ministry. The only thing that really matters for Paul is that Jesus was crucified and then raised from the dead. As Paul says in his letter of First 1 Corinthians, "All that I knew among you was Christ and him crucified." For Paul, it was the death and resurrection that brought salvation from sin. So, in the opinion of some scholars, Paul transformed the simple religion of Jesus into the religion about Jesus, thereby creating Christianity.

I'm not going to say that I agree with this particular opinion because, in fact, I don't think that Paul is the one who invented the idea that Christ died for the sins of the world. He is, though, the one who popularized this view, and spread this view throughout the Mediterranean world, and was more responsible than anyone else that we know of for creating Christianity as a major world religion, as opposed to a sect within Judaism. To that extent, of course, Paul was extremely important. So it's important for us to know something about Paul and his writings.

Unfortunately, we're not in a good situation when it comes to knowing about Paul's life because the sources for Paul's life are rather sparse. In fact, there are two kinds of sources. First, there's the book of Acts, which I mentioned in my previous lecture. The book of Acts is the account of the spread of Christianity throughout the Mediterranean world after Jesus' death. Paul figures prominently in the book of Acts. In chapter 9, we have an account of Paul converting to Christianity and then, we have an account throughout the rest of the book of Acts, chapters 9–28, of Paul's activity in converting other people to faith in Christ—Paul as a missionary. The problem is that the book of Acts, which gives a historical account of Paul's life, sometimes stands in conflict with what Paul himself has to say in his letters. So that many scholars are not convinced that the book of Acts can be taken as an objectively verifiable account of the activities of the apostle Paul; which means, for the most part, we're restricted to Paul's letters when trying to understand what Paul was all about.

Still, there are 13 letters in Paul's name in the New Testament, and so that should be a good source of information for Paul. Again, there's a problem though, the one I pointed out in the last lecture. Namely, that of the 13 letters that go under Paul's name in the New Testament, only seven of them are undisputedly Pauline. The other six may have been written by followers of Paul. To understand Paul, we are more or less restricted to seven letters that Paul wrote that are contained in the New Testament.

From these letters, supplemented with some information from the book of Acts, we can acquire important information about the life and the teachings of Paul. One of the most important things to note is that Paul did not start out as a follower of Jesus. Paul was not one of Jesus' disciples and, in fact, Paul probably did not know the earthly Jesus. It appears that Paul did not grow up in Palestine. He was probably about Jesus' age, but he grew up outside of Palestine in what's called the Jewish Diaspora, the dispersion of the Jews throughout the Mediterranean. Paul's native language was not Aramaic, as Jesus' was; Paul's native language was Greek. Paul does tell us that he was a very religious Jew prior to becoming a follower of Jesus; in fact, he was an avid Pharisee. This is an interesting datum because we don't have writings from Pharisees from the days of Jesus or immediately thereafter. Within the first century, we have very few writings from any Pharisees. The earliest writing from any Pharisee we have happens to be the writings of Paul, who converted away from being a Jewish Pharisee to being a Jew who believed in Jesus.

What we learn from Paul's letters is that he was an avid Pharisaic Jew who started out not following Jesus, but persecuting Jesus' followers. Why would Paul, as an avid Jew, have persecuted Jesus' followers before he himself converted to be a follower of Jesus? Unfortunately, Paul doesn't actually tell us why it is he persecuted the early Christians, only that he did so. We're left somewhat to speculation, but it doesn't take too much to understand why it is that Paul found the Christian claims about Jesus to be offensive, so offensive that they deserved to be persecuted.

The early Christians maintained that Jesus was the Jewish Messiah who had died for the sins of the world. In the modern day, most people think of the Messiah as somebody who has to die for the sins of the world. At least, that's certainly what Christians think; that's what the Messiah was supposed to do—die for the sins of the world. Prior to Christianity, however, we don't know of any Jew who thought that the Messiah was someone who had to be executed or would be somebody who would be raised from the dead.

Jews had a variety of understandings of what the Messiah would be like in the first century. Most Jews probably didn't anticipate a Messiah at all, just as most Jews today are not looking out for a Messiah. But, there were some Jews who anticipated a coming Messiah in the first century. The Jews who expected a coming Messiah had a variety of expectations of what this Messiah would be like. Some thought he'd be a great warrior figure, like King David of old. They thought he might be a son of David, a descendant of David who would be a warrior figure who would oppose God's enemies violently and overthrow the oppressive forces, which were the Romans, who were occupying the land of Israel. The Messiah would drive out the opposing Roman forces and would set up a kingdom in Jerusalem, a sovereign Israelite state in Jerusalem. He'd be a mighty warrior, a political figure. Other Jews anticipated that the Messiah would be a figure who would come from Heaven as a Heavenly being who would overthrow God's enemies and set up God's kingdom on earth. Other Jews expected that the Messiah would be a great priest-like figure who, with great authority, would interpret the law of Moses for his people in the coming kingdom of God. There were a variety of expectations of what the Messiah would be like among Jews in the first century; but there was no expectation that the Messiah would be a crucified criminal. In fact, all of the views of the Messiah shared one thing in common; they shared the view that the Messiah would be a person of grandeur and power.

Who was Jesus? Was he a person of grandeur and power? Was he a warrior who overthrew the Romans? Was he a savior who came on the clouds of

Heaven and overthrew the forces of evil? Was he a great priest who interpreted the law in an authoritative way? Quite the contrary, Jesus was an itinerant preacher from a small backwoods part of the empire, from a little town that nobody had ever heard of, Nazareth, who got in trouble with the law and got crucified by the Romans. Jesus was a crucified criminal. To call Jesus the Messiah simply didn't make sense to most Jews of the first century.

Christians, though, insisted that Jesus was the Messiah. Well, how could he be the Messiah if he wasn't a figure of grandeur and power? According to Christians, the Messiah first had to suffer, and then he would rule in power. The way they came to understand Jesus as the Messiah was by reading the Jewish scriptures and finding passages in the Jewish scripture that talk about one of God's righteous ones suffering for the sins of others. Especially passages like Isaiah 53 or Psalms 22. These passages, however, which continue to be quoted by Christians today, never refer to the Messiah. They refer to some figure that is persecuted, who is killed; but they don't call this person the Messiah; so most Jews did not interpret these passages messianically, in reference to the Messiah.

Christians, though, came to think that these passages in the Old Testament were referring to a future Messiah, even though the passages didn't talk about the Messiah. They claimed they were referring to the Messiah; Jews said they weren't. Christians, then, concluded that Jesus, since he was the Messiah and since he suffered, was the suffering Messiah and, therefore, they concluded that the Messiah must suffer. This view made no sense to most Jews.

Now, I get in trouble every year when I do this in front of my class of undergraduates, but to give you a sense of the emotional response that most Jews had to the claim that Jesus is the Messiah, I'll give you an analogy. It would be like my telling you that I think David Koresh is the lord of the universe. David Koresh—the guy at Waco that got killed with the Branch Davidians? Yeah, yeah, he's the lord of the universe. He's not the lord of the universe, he was a crook, and a criminal, and he's probably a sexual offender, and he gathered arms, and he was violent. No, no, no—he's the lord of the universe. Now, the kind of reaction we have to saying that David Koresh is the lord of the universe is the reaction that most Jews had to the claim that Jesus was the Messiah. He wasn't the Messiah; he was crucified by the Romans. I get in trouble, as I said, every year for saying this. I always get these teaching evaluations that come back that say, "I can't believe that Ehrman thinks that David Koresh is the lord of the universe."

I'm not saying that that's what I think, but that's the kind of reaction that most Jews had. That probably was the reaction that the apostle Paul had. Calling Jesus the Messiah was wrong and blasphemous because Jesus was a lowly, crucified criminal; and so Paul persecuted the Christians until one of the greatest turnarounds in all of religious history, when the apostle Paul converted from being a persecutor of the Christian Church to being its greatest advocate and missionary.

What converted Paul? It appears that Paul had some kind of visionary experience of Christ in the course of his own persecution of Christians. I don't know exactly what happened, but Paul indicates that he had a vision of the resurrected Jesus; that Jesus actually appeared to him as living, even though Paul knew that he was dead. This vision of Jesus after his death, Paul interpreted as evidence that Jesus had been raised by God from the dead. But, if God raised Jesus from the dead, that must mean that Jesus is not cursed by God, as one who is crucified; he's the one blessed by God.

This vision of Jesus changed everything for Paul. It changed his understanding of Jesus. Jesus must be the one under God's blessing, but then why would he have died on a cross? Paul starts reasoning backwards. He has, as a given, his experience of Jesus as a living being. That means he must have been raised. He starts reasoning backwards. That means his death must not have been just a miscarriage of justice, or the death of a prophet, or a deserved death at the hands of the Romans. The death must have had some kind of divine purpose for it. Why, then, would Jesus die? If he stands under God's blessing, he must not have died for anything that he did wrong. Maybe, then, he died for the sins of others.

Paul's backward reasoning leads him to think that the death of Jesus was a death that brings salvation to others, as is verified by the fact that God raised him from the dead. That means that Jesus' death is the way that God deals with the problem of sin. All people are guilty before God of committing sins. Sin controls people; people act sinfully. But Christ died for sins, so that if a person puts their faith in Christ's death, their sins are covered over. Christ's death brings a right relationship, a right standing, before God. This is Paul's backward reasoning. When I say backwards, I don't mean that in a negative way. I mean he's reasoning in reverse from his experience in Christ's resurrection.

If a right standing before God comes by Jesus' death, then what about the Jewish religion? In the Jewish religion, God has given the Law of Moses to the Jews to follow. The Law shows that people are in a right standing before

God. God gave his law to his people, the Law of Moses, the Torah as it's called—the books of the Old Testament where you find the laws of Moses. Surely, keeping these laws is what makes a person in a right standing before God, or at least shows that a person is one of God's chosen people? Right? Paul came to think that that was wrong. Even though he had been an avid Jew, an avid follower of the Law, he came to realize that following the Law cannot put a person in a right standing before God; only Christ's death can put a person in a right standing before God. This means that all people can be in a right standing before God by having faith in Christ, not by keeping the Law.

Now, I don't want to say that Paul stopped being a Jew. I don't think that Paul stopped being a Jew any more than Jesus stopped being a Jew. Paul continued to be a Jew. He probably continued to keep the Jewish law; but Paul did not think that keeping the Jewish Law had any bearing on one's standing before God. Whether a person was a Jew or a non-Jew (a Gentile), a person could be right with God not by keeping the Law, but by having faith in Christ.

One other effect of Paul's belief that Jesus was raised from the dead was that Paul came to believe that, on the basis of this resurrection, the end of time was near. Paul was a Jewish Pharisee who, like other Jewish Pharisees and other Jews, believed that he was living at the end of the age. Many Jews in the first century believed that the end of time was near and that at the end of this age, God would raise people from the dead, and they would face judgment. Those who had sided with God would be rewarded; those who had opposed God would be punished. This would happen at the end of this age.

What is Paul to think once he comes to believe that Jesus was raised from the dead? Well, the resurrection has started. Jesus is raised as the "first fruits," as Paul says in the book of 1 Corinthians. That's an agricultural image. The "first fruits" refers to the time of the harvest. When you go out the first day, you bring in the first fruits, and then you have a celebration that night because the harvest has begun. When is the rest of the harvest brought in? You go back out the next day. Once the resurrection has started, it's going to come about in a big way. Paul, therefore, concluded that he was living at the end of time, and he thought that Jesus himself would return in power to the earth, in glory as the coming Messiah, and that this would happen within his own lifetime. Paul appears to have thought that the end would come while he was still living, as we'll see in a later lecture, especially in First Thessalonians, Paul's earliest writing.

Once Paul became convinced that Jesus was raised from the dead, and that Jesus' death is what brought salvation from sin, he began proclaiming his new faith in Jesus, so that he turned from being a persecutor of the Church to being a proclaimer of the Gospel. Paul began proclaiming that Jesus was the one who could restore people to a right standing before God. All of this was based on his visionary experience of Christ's resurrection. With the help of other fellow converts, Paul began establishing churches. He saw himself, principally, as the missionary to the Gentiles, or the apostle to the Gentiles. In other words, Paul was principally concerned, not with converting other Jews to faith; he was concerned about converting pagans to the faith. The word "pagan," in this context, I should point out, doesn't mean what it usually means today; like when I refer to my next-door neighbor as a real pagan, which he is, by the way. Instead, the word "pagan," in this context, is used simply to refer to anybody in the ancient world who is neither a Jew, nor a Christian; someone who is not a monotheist, but is a polytheist. Paganism represents all of the polytheistic religions throughout the Roman Empire; and virtually everybody, of course, was a polytheist, believing in many gods.

Paul's mission was to convert people from believing in many gods to believing that there's only one God, and that Jesus is his son, whose death can bring a right standing before God, so that a person can have eternal life. Paul's mission, then, was to convert pagans. As I pointed out in the last lecture, Paul went from one urban setting to another, in order to establish churches—churches of people who came to believe in the one true God and his son Jesus. As soon as Paul would establish worshipping communities in one location, then he would go to another location and start communities there; and as he would hear of problems in his various churches that he left behind, he would write them letters in order to help them deal with their problems.

What about these letters of Paul? Let me say something about what it meant to write a letter in the ancient world. On the assumption that Paul was writing letters to his churches, what exactly did that mean in the ancient world before you had the U.S. Postal Service? In the ancient world, letters were a very common form of communication. Most commonly, letters were dictated rather than written out by hand. The reason they were dictated was because the vast majority of people couldn't write. It appears that Paul could write; he could at least sign his name, because it looks like in some of his letters, he actually must have made the signature at the end and penned a few words, so they would come from his own hand. But most of Paul's letters appear to have been dictated.

These letters that were dictated could have been written either on papyrus—an ancient writing material made out of a reed-like substance, the papyrus stalk—or sometimes, they were written on wax tablets. It was popular to write letters on wax tablets. You'd have a board that had a hollowed-out center with wax poured inside, and you would write the letter in the wax using a sharp stylus. Then when the person got the letter, they would send a letter back by smoothing over the wax and then using it again; so it was reusable writing material.

Most often, letters were not sent through the mail, since there was no mail service per se; they were hand delivered by somebody who was going to wherever the recipient lived. Usually the letters, once they were read, were destroyed, so the substance could be used once again. If there was any reason to keep the letter, though, the letter would be copied by hand and it would then be circulated more broadly. This is what happened with at least seven of Paul's letters; they were copied by hand and then more broadly circulated. These letters were meant to be read aloud to his communities. When Paul wrote a letter to a church, not everyone in the church would read a copy because most people couldn't read. Somebody who could read would read the thing aloud to the entire community.

These letters, by and large, are written to deal with problems of Paul's churches. These were problems involving both how to live and what to believe. A clear example of a letter that is concerned with how a Christian should live is Paul's first letter to the Corinthians. When you read First Corinthians, it becomes clear that the Corinthians were experiencing numerous problems in their congregations. There were divisions in the churches; people weren't getting along. There were factions in the churches that were so bad that some Corinthian Christians were taking other Corinthian Christians to court. There were instances of flagrant sexual immorality. There were men who were visiting prostitutes and then bragging about it afterwards in church. There was one guy who was actually living with his stepmother, which Paul thought was a very bad idea.

There were other ethical kinds of dilemmas; for example, the question of whether it was right to eat meat that had been sacrificed to a pagan god. They would sacrifice an animal to a pagan god, and then sell the meat. The god couldn't do anything with it, so they would sell the meat. Is it right to eat that meat, or by doing so, are you participating in pagan idolatry?

There were issues about the worship services, and how these worship services should be conducted. Apparently, the worship services in Corinth were rather chaotic. Paul deals with all of these questions through 1 Corinthians one by one, saying he knows what the problem is, and then giving his pastoral advice about what to do about the problem. It's clear that in this letter, as with the other letters, what Paul writes, is to stand in for his own apostolic presence, because he simply couldn't be everywhere at once. So, he would write these letters to give his insights and advice to churches. That would be an example of a letter concerned with lifestyle.

An example of a letter concerned with Christian belief would be Paul's letter to the Galatians. The letter to the Galatians is concerned more with doctrinal issues than ethical issues. The question that Galatians address is this: Since Jesus is the Jewish Messiah, sent from the Jewish God, to the Jewish people, in fulfillment of the Jewish Law, doesn't a person have to be Jewish to be a follower of Jesus? That's the question the Galatians had, and they were taking this question to some extreme. The converted pagans and the Galatian community were becoming Jews to follow Jesus, which meant that the men were getting circumcised, which by all accounts, was not a pleasant operation. Paul hears of this situation and he goes ballistic. Galatians is an angry letter; it's the only letter from Paul's hand that does not begin by Paul thanking God for the congregation. Paul thinks that the Galatians have gotten it completely wrong, because they think that the person has to keep the Law to be right with God, whereas the Law cannot make a person right with God; only faith in Christ can make a person right with God. Therefore, Paul writes Galatians to warn them not to be circumcised, not to keep the Jewish law, because doing so will only show that they have fallen from the grace of God that comes by faith in Jesus' death, which is the only way a person can be right with God.

To sum up, by reading Paul's letters, we can get a sense of the kinds of problems that the earliest Christian communities were experiencing, as well as a sense of the teachings and theology of Paul himself, which will be the subject of our next lecture.

Lecture Three
The Pauline Epistles

Scope: Now that we have some understanding about how literature was produced and disseminated in the ancient world, we can turn to the Pauline Epistles themselves to get a sense of what these, our earliest surviving Christian writings, were all about. As we will see, all of Paul's letters were *occasional* in nature—that is, they were written not in order to expound Paul's ideas in a vacuum but to address specific problems and issues that had arisen in his communities, problems related to what his fellow Christians should believe and how they should live. In this lecture, we will consider some of the major teachings of Paul's Epistles and see how he shaped his theological and ethical views in light of the problems that had emerged in his burgeoning Christian communities.

Outline

I. We have already started to examine the life and teachings of the apostle Paul, based on the materials preserved in the New Testament.

   A. These are our earliest and most accurate accounts: From later writings, we can learn how legends about him developed, but we have nothing from his own hand outside the New Testament.

   B. In this lecture, we will consider at greater length some of the key teachings of Paul and see how they came to expression in two of his important letters, the letter to the Romans and his first letter to the Thessalonians.

II. In some ways, the letter to the Romans is the best place to turn to get a sense of Paul's overarching gospel message.

   A. All of Paul's other letters were *occasional* (that is, motivated by certain situations that had arisen) and directed to his own churches.

   B. The letter to the Romans is addressed to a church that Paul did not found and had never visited.

C. The occasion for the letter is indicated in its beginning and ending.

    1. Paul was about to make a missionary trip to the western parts of the empire and wanted to use the Roman church as his base of operation.

    2. But the Christians in Rome had heard some negative things about Paul (which shows that he was not everywhere regarded as a leading apostolic spokesperson).

III. The letter to the Romans then lays out Paul's understanding of the Christian Gospel.

    A. In some ways, the Gospel is predicated on "bad news" that is antecedent to the good news.

        1. The bad news is that everyone, whether Jew or Gentile, is estranged from God, and there is nothing that anyone—even good, law-abiding Jews—can do to change the situation.

        2. Pagans, even though they know there is only one true God, reject God; Jews, who have the Law of God, break the Law and are, therefore, no better than pagans.

        3. There is no problem with the Law, only with people who are forced, by sin, to act contrary to God's will.

        4. The penalty for breaking God's Law is to be alienated from God, and the Law can't solve that problem.

    B. The good news is that God himself has changed it by having Christ die for the sins of others.

        1. Christ's death brings a reconciliation between God and his estranged people.

        2. It also empowers people to do what they could not be empowered to do in any other way (for example, by keeping the Law): to overcome the power of sin to which they were enslaved.

    C. This teaching does not negate the teaching of the Jewish Law.

        1. In fact, according to Paul, his proclamation of faith in Christ upholds the teaching of the Law.

        2. This can be seen above all in the story of Abraham, the "father of the Jews," who was made right with God by faith, not by following the Law: Abraham was made right with God *before* he was given the Law about circumcision, meaning that circumcision is not necessary for a right standing with God.

3. Paul uses this example to show that salvation comes not by Law but by having faith in the promise of God, which is fulfilled by Christ's death.
   4. As a result, Paul did not see himself as standing in opposition to the Jewish people, whom God would eventually save as they came to believe in the messiah God had sent.

D. Finally, even though salvation comes apart from the Law, this is not a proclamation that leads to lawlessness. Quite the contrary, those made right with God through Christ will be the ones empowered to do what God wants.

E. This, in sum, is Paul's teaching of justification by faith, apart from the works of the Law.
   1. It was this teaching that stands at the heart of everything else that he said and did on his mission to convert others.
   2. But most of his letters in fact deal with different issues, as these had arisen in his communities.

IV. This can be seen in his earliest letter, to the Thessalonians.

A. Paul had converted a group of pagans in the city of Thessalonica to belief in the one God and in Jesus, his son, who had died and been raised from the dead.

B. He also taught them that Christ would soon return in judgment on the earth and to bring in God's kingdom.

C. But after he left the community, some of its members had died, leading to considerable anxiety among those who were left behind: Does this mean that those who died before the kingdom had arrived had "lost out" on a chance to inherit salvation?

D. Paul's letter is written to address this question.
   1. In it, he reaffirms his faith in the death and resurrection of Jesus.
   2. And he gives the congregation further instruction: Those who died in Christ have not at all lost out on the promises; when Christ returns, it is they who will rise first to meet him in the air.
   3. Then, all believers who are still alive will join them, entering into Christ's eternal kingdom.
   4. This teaching is rooted in belief in a three-story universe: The dead are below us, and God is above us.

5. It also presupposes that the original expectation of the imminent end of the world was starting to cause some frustration among believers.

E. Paul, though, as always, worked out the implications of his gospel message for the crisis at hand, showing how in Christ God had fulfilled and would yet fulfill all his promises, by raising the dead.

V. Paul's letters were all written to speak to situations in the churches he was addressing, but at the heart of every letter, in one way or another, is his fundamental gospel message: that it was through the death and resurrection of Jesus that God had restored people to a right relationship with himself.

Essential Reading:

Bart D. Ehrman, *A Brief Introduction to the New Testament*, chapters 13 and 16.

Calvin Roetzel, *The Letters of Paul: Conversations in Context.*

Supplementary Reading:

Gerald Hawthorne and Ralph Martin, *Dictionary of Paul and His Letters.*

Leander Keck, *Paul and His Letters.*

A. J. M. Wedderburn, *The Reasons for Romans.*

Questions to Consider:

1. Try to imagine what Paul's Christian opponents might have said about his Gospel to make the Romans suspicious of him. Is there anything in his proclamation that could be caricatured to make Paul's message appear dangerous to believers?

2. Do you think Paul anticipated that the "end" would still not have come, now nearly 2,000 years later?

Lecture Three—Transcript
The Pauline Epistles

We've already started to examine the life and teachings of the apostle Paul, based on the materials preserved in the New Testament. These New Testament letters of Paul are our earliest and most accurate accounts. From later writings outside the New Testament, we can learn how legends about Paul developed, but we have nothing from his own hand outside the New Testament. As I mentioned in the previous lecture, we have seven letters that are indisputably by Paul within the New Testament, seven of the 13 letters that go under his name. These seven are Romans, First and Second Corinthians, Galatians, Philippians, First Thessalonians, and Philemon. Sometimes it's easy to confuse these letters because the message in them sometimes is very similar. But scholars, of course, try to differentiate among the letters, to keep clear what is in each one because each letter is written to address a different situation and, therefore, has a different message.

The problem of confusing Paul's letter, though, sometimes is palpable. I have a friend who was once asked to deliver a scripture reading at a funeral, a very common funeral reading comes from the letters of Paul, from Second Corinthians, chapter 5, where Paul is talking about what happens to the body once it dies; how God provides another body for the person who has died. The passage is Second Corinthians, chapter 5, verse 1, where Paul says, "For we know that if the earthly tent we live in is destroyed, we have a building from God, a house not made with hands eternal in the heavens." My friend who got up to read the scripture at this funeral, though, unfortunately opened his text not to Second Corinthians, chapter 5, but to First Corinthians, chapter 5, and read the following. First Corinthians chapter 5, verse 1: "It is actually reported that there is sexual immorality among you, and of a kind that is not found even among pagans. For a man is living with his father's wife." Not knowing what to do, my friend reasoned that probably people weren't paying attention anyway, so he read it reverently and sat down. It's a good thing not to confuse what Paul says in his various letters because each was written in a different situation to a different context.

In some ways the best place to turn to understand Paul's overarching Gospel message is his letter to the Romans. The first part of this lecture will be dealing with Paul's letter to the Romans. It's an unusual letter in a number of ways. All of the other letters of Paul, as I've intimated, were occasional letters, by which I mean that the letters were motivated by certain situations that had arisen in Paul's churches, so he writes to address these various occasions. Romans is a little different because Romans is not addressed to a church that Paul had founded; in fact Paul indicates in his letter to the Romans that he had never even visited the church in Rome. He's not then writing to solve the problems of what to believe and how to act in Romans; he's writing for some other occasion.

The occasion for the letter of the Romans is indicated at the beginning and ending of the Epistle. As it becomes clear once reading Romans, chapter 1, and Romans, chapters 15 and 16, Paul was about to make a missionary trip to the western part of the Roman Empire. He evidently wanted to use the church in the city of Rome as a kind of base of operation for his westward mission. He intends on taking the Gospel further west all the way to Spain, and so he needs a base of operation, and he wants that to be Rome. But the Christians in Rome had heard some negative things about Paul and his mission.

Paul, then, is writing in order to clear up the matter, so that they will support him in his missionary work. This may seem odd to us today that somebody would think badly of Paul, but it's because we think of Paul as so important for the history of Christianity. We need to realize that in his own day Paul was a highly controversial figure. We know Paul was a controversial figure because in virtually everyone of his letters, he talks about his Christian opponents—people who had opposing points of view.

For example, as I mentioned briefly in the previous lecture, his letter to the Galatians. The Galatians think that in order to be true followers of Jesus, they, like Jesus need to be Jewish. They didn't come up with this idea themselves. We learned from the letter of the Galatians that in fact other Christian missionaries had visited the churches in Galatia and had told them this, had told them that, in fact, this is the understanding of Jesus' own apostles in Jerusalem, and that Paul has presented a fabricated Gospel. Paul then writes Galatians to set the record straight, to show that he has the right Gospel and his opponents have the wrong Gospel. Paul had opponents in Galatia, and it wasn't just Galatia; Paul had opponents in a number of places. Most of his letters indicate that he had Christian opponents.

The Romans had heard some things about Paul and they aren't sure that they can trust him. Paul needs their trust and support, though, and so he writes them a letter in which he spells out in the clearest fashion possible the nature of his proclamation. This is to dispel any negative feelings that the Romans have towards him and towards his alleged message. The occasion of Romans makes an ideal place to look at and understand what Paul's message was, because he's trying to explain his message so that it won't be misunderstood.

In this lecture I want to talk about what Paul's message was, as found in the book of Romans. In some ways Paul's Gospel, his proclamation of good news, is predicated on a set of bad news. The bad news is that everybody is alienated from God and there's nothing they can do about it. That's bad news, indeed, if you're a religious person, to find out that you are, in fact, not God's ally but God's enemy. That's the bad news that is the basis for Paul's Gospel. As Paul says in Romans chapter 1, verse 18, "The wrath of God is revealed from heaven against all ungodliness and wickedness of those who by their wickedness suppress the truth." Who are these people who suppress the truth?

Paul goes on to show that pagans, in other words those who are polytheists, worship many gods because they've rejected the knowledge of the one true God. According to Paul, even those who are polytheists, the pagans of the Roman Empire, knew that, in fact, there's only one God; but they rejected that knowledge, and thereby, became idolaters. "For what can be known about God is plain to them because God has shown it to them. Ever since the creation of the world his eternal power and divine nature have been understood and seen through the things He had made."

Paul indicates that people can look around the world and understand that this world, this creation requires a creator. There is only one God who created this world; and therefore Paul says, "They are without excuse. For though they knew God, they did not honor Him as God, or give Him thanks, but they became futile in their thinking, and their senseless minds were darkened. Claiming to be wise, they became fools." Then he goes on to indicate that that's why polytheists began worshipping mortal humans, or birds, or four-footed animals, or reptiles. And because they started worshipping these other so-called gods, God gave them up to live immoral and unethical lives. As a footnote, pagans were not really wild and profligate any more than anybody else is. Pagans in the ancient world were just as moral as most people are today; but as a Jew who's now a believer in Jesus, Paul is condemning the outsiders, the pagans, for what he considers to be their rank immorality. Why are they so immoral? Because they rejected God, and therefore, God rejected them.

Okay, so pagans are standing under the wrath of God. What about Jews? Jews have God's Law. Jews know better than to worship the idols. Therefore aren't they on God's side? Paul turns in [Romans], chapter 2, verse 1, then, to address the Jews, and he says, "Therefore you have no excuse, whoever you are, when you judge others; for in passing judgment on another, you condemn yourself, because you, the judge, are doing the very same things." He goes on to indicate that even Jews who have the Law of God, break the Law of God. Since they break the Law of God, they are no better than the rank pagans who are idolaters.

He goes on to say, "If you call yourself a Jew, and rely on the Law, and boast of your relationship with God, and know his will, and determine what's best because you're instructed in the Law; and if you're sure that you are a guide to the blind, a light to those are in darkness, you then that teach others, will you not teach yourself? You who forbid adultery, do you not commit adultery? You who boast in the Law, do you not dishonor God by breaking the Law?"

Paul indicates that, in fact, the Law of God itself indicates that everybody breaks the Law. He goes on in [Romans], chapter 3, verse 9, "Are we [who are Jews] any better off [than the pagans]? No, not at all; for we have charged that all [people], both Jews and Greeks, are under the power of sin. For 'there is no one who is righteous, not even one.'" Here he's quoting scripture. "There's no one who understands, there's no one who seeks after God." Scripture itself indicates that not even Jews are right before God. He concludes this bad news segment of his gospel by saying, "For no human being will be justified in God's sight by doing the deeds prescribed by the Law, for through the Law comes the knowledge of sin."

Some people might have argued, look Paul, we are Jews who have God's Law. God gave us this Law because we're his chosen people. By following his Law we show we're his chosen people. Paul's view is, yes you have the Law but you don't keep the Law. In fact, this is common knowledge that people could not actually keep the Law, because that's why the Law prescribed sacrifices for sins. In the temple in Jerusalem the Jewish priests would offer sacrifices for the sins of the people. That presupposes that people have sins for which sacrifices are necessary. The Law, then, provides some remedy for sin; but the point is, that means that people sin and violate God's Law, as indicated in the Law itself.

The problem with the Law for Paul is not that the Law is bad; in fact, the Law is good. The Law is God's will. The Law tells people who God is, how he expects to be worshipped, and how he can be obeyed. That's good. There's no problem with the Law. The problem is with people. People are empowered by an alien force that Paul calls sin. Sin is a power in the world that enslaves people and forces them to do things contrary to God's will. The Law can't do anything about that. Sin drives people to break God's Law, requiring, therefore, sacrifices. The Law is good, but the Law can't do anything about the fact that people break the Law. Paul indicates that it doesn't matter if you try to keep the Law, you still are alienated from God.

It's like this: If you've broken one law, for example, you've murdered somebody, you can't get right with the government by saying, "Yeah, but I kept all the other laws." You can keep all the other laws, but if you've broken one of the laws, you're guilty. It's that way with the Law before God; you break a law, and it doesn't matter if you keep all the other laws, or how well you keep the other laws; you've broken the Law, and there's a penalty. The penalty for Paul is that people are alienated from God, and the Law can't solve that problem.

How is the problem solved? This is where Paul's Gospel comes into play. Paul thinks that God himself has solved the problem that people are alienated from him. He solved the problem of alienation, not through the Law, but apart from the Law. Romans, chapter 3, verse 21: "But now, apart from law, the righteousness of God has been disclosed…the righteousness of God through faith in Jesus Christ for all who believe."

Paul goes on to say that everybody, whether Jew or Gentile, is alienated from God because of sin, but God has taken care of the sin problem by having Jesus die on the cross. All people are now justified or made right with God by his grace as a gift through the redemption that is in Christ Jesus. It's Jesus' death that puts a person in a right standing before God. The way it works is, Jesus himself died, not for his own sins, but for the sins of others. Everybody else has committed sins, and keeping the Law won't do anything about that. Jesus' death, however, allows a person to be right with God because Jesus' death atoned for sins, or covered over sins. The way a person is right with God, then, is by claiming that atonement for themselves. In other words, by having faith in Jesus' death, a person's sins are covered over by the blood of the cross. As a result, then, people can be made right with God, not by being Jewish, not by keeping the Jewish Law, but by having faith in Jesus. It doesn't matter whether a person is a Jew or a Gentile, all have equally sinned, and all are equally made right with God through Jesus' death, which brings a reconciliation with God.

It's important to see that Paul remains Jewish. He still thinks the Jewish Law is given by the Jewish God to the Jewish people; but since people have violated the Law, God has done something else in order to put them in a right standing with him, so that all people, whether Jew or Gentile, have to be made right with God, not through the Law, but through the death of Jesus. This creates a kind of irony for Paul's thinking because, according to Paul, the Law itself teaches that salvation does not come by the Law. It's kind of ironic.

According to Paul, the Law itself teaches that the Law cannot bring about salvation, and he has a number of proofs for this. One of the proofs that he uses in the book of Romans has to do with the father of the Jews, Abraham. In the first book of the Torah, Genesis 15:6, we're told that God makes a promise to Abraham that he's going to have many descendants. Even though he's an old man, and his wife is an old woman, and they don't have any children, God promises Abraham they'll have many descendants. We're told in Genesis 15:6 that Abraham believed God, and it was counted to him as righteousness. Paul asks how Abraham is made right with God? How does he have righteousness or right standing before by God by believing God—not by doing anything, but simply by having faith in God's promise? When did Abraham get the Jewish rite of circumcision? When was Abraham told that he and his descendants needed to be circumcised as the sign of the right standing before God? In Genesis, chapter 17, Paul notes that Abraham was made right with God before he was given circumcision. His conclusion is that being right with God is apart from circumcision, that circumcision is not necessary for a right standing before God. The Law came after Abraham was made right with God; therefore, the Law is not necessary for a right standing before God. Paul uses the example of Abraham from the Law itself in order to show that salvation comes not by Law, but by having faith in the promise of God. How is the promise fulfilled? The promise is fulfilled when Christ dies on the cross for Paul.

That's Paul's understanding of his Gospel. It's an understanding that is typically called "Paul's Doctrine of Justification by Faith" (being made right with God by faith), or the fuller title is, "Justification by Faith Apart from Works of the Law." All people, Jew or Gentile, are made right with God by faith in God's promise fulfilled in the death of Jesus, not by keeping the Law. Even though salvation comes apart from the Law, Paul insists that his proclamation does not lead to lawlessness. In other words, even though a person is made right with God apart from the Law, it doesn't mean people can thereby start going out and start breaking the Law. If the Law says, don't commit adultery, it means it; you shouldn't commit adultery. If it says, don't murder, you shouldn't murder. If it says, don't bear false witness, you shouldn't bear false witness. You should obey the ethical prescriptions of the Law because being made right with God does not lead to lawlessness, even though this being made right with God is apart from the Law.

Paul spends a good deal of Romans arguing that people need to lead ethical lives by following God's prescriptions for action as found in the Law. Even though doing that won't make you right with God, if you are right with God, you'll do that. Paul argues for an ethical lifestyle. This then is Paul's teaching of "Justification by Faith Apart from Works of the Law." This teaching of Paul's own justification is the teaching that stands at the heart of everything else that he said and did on his mission to convert others. When he converted pagans, he converted them to this particular belief. As it turns out, though, most of Paul's letters deal with other issues; they don't deal with this issue of how to be right with God. Only really Romans and Galatians deals with that. The other letters deal with other situations that had arisen in Paul's churches.

I want, in the second part of my lecture, to talk about one of these other letters, to show you how Paul writes his letters, and how he incorporates his views into them. I've chosen the earliest that Paul wrote, the first letter to the Thessalonians. This is Paul's earliest letter. It's usually dated around AD 49 or 50, so we're talking about 20 years after Jesus' death. It is the first Christian writing of any kind that we have. When you read 1 Thessalonians, it becomes clear that Paul had established the church in the city of Thessalonica by converting former pagans to believe in Christ. So he talks about how he turned them from worshipping idols to worshipping the one, true God. Paul established this community of former pagans, then, to become believers in Jesus. He left the community, and what happened after he left is that some of the members of the community had died, which raised considerable anxiety among those who were left behind.

It's not quite clear what they were anxious about, but it appears that Paul had taught his converts that they were living at the end of time, and that Jesus would soon return from Heaven to establish his kingdom. Remember, in my previous lecture, I pointed out that because Paul believed in the resurrection, he thought that the resurrection had started already and that Christ would return soon from Heaven and there would be a general resurrection. Those who had died would be raised; those who were on God side would be rewarded; those who were opposed to God would be punished; then the world would enter into an eternal kingdom of God. Paul appears to have taught the Thessalonians that this was going to happen right away, but some people died, and this upset the Thessalonians. Does this mean that the people who died have lost out on the benefits of Christ's kingdom that is soon to come?

First Thessalonians is written, in large part, in order to address this particular question, the question, what about people who have already died? Have they lost out? The key passage is in chapter 4, verse 13, and following, where Paul says, "We would not have you ignorant, brothers and sisters..." (Or if you put the comma in the other place it would be, "We would not have you, ignorant brothers and sisters...") "about those who have died so that you may not grieve as others who have no hope. For since we believe that Jesus died and rose again, even so, through him, God will bring with him those who have died." This is where it gets very interesting: "For this we declare to you by a word of the Lord, that we who are alive, who are left, until the coming of the Lord, will by no means precede those who have died." Notice that Paul seems to think he's going to be alive when Jesus returns. Verse 16: "For the Lord himself, with a cry of command, with the archangels' call and the sound of God's trumpet, will descend from Heaven, and the dead in Christ will rise first. Then we who are alive, who are left, will be caught up in the clouds together with them to meet the Lord in the air. And so we will be with the Lord forever. Therefore, encourage one another with these words."

In the context, this teaching is to be comforting to those who are worried about those who died. Paul, some people have died and so have they lost out? No, they haven't lost out, when Christ returns in glory, in fact, the dead will rise first. Paul's scenario is that Christ is going to come back from Heaven on the clouds. People who have died who have believed in Christ are going to be raised from the dead, and they're going to sort of zap up into Heaven and meet Jesus in the air. Then people who are alive who are believing in Jesus are also going to be sucked up, sort of in the aftermath, and they're going to meet Jesus in the air; and they're going to live forever in this heavenly airy, heavenly kingdom. This is the passage that fundamentalist Christians refer to when they talk about the "rapture." I should point out that the term "rapture" doesn't occur in this passage, and the term "rapture" in fact never occurs in the New Testament; it's not a biblical word. Moreover, this idea of Christ coming back and people being raised to meet him up in the air is not found in the Book of Revelation, which most people who believe in the rapture don't realize, that it's not taught there at all. It does seem to be taught here in First Thessalonians, chapter 4.

It's important to recognize that this teaching is predicated on the notion of a three-storied universe, which was a common notion among some Jews in antiquity. The world we live in is in three stories. Below us is the realm of the dead; we are in the realm of the living; and above us is the realm of God. As you know, in the book of Genesis, when God creates the heavens and the earth, he puts a firmament between the waters beneath and the waters above, so that people, and animals, and plants live on this firmament. This is a firm substance that separates the waters above the firmament from the waters below the firmament. That's why, when the flood comes with Noah in the book of Genesis, the flood actually is waters coming up from beneath and waters coming down from above. The world is returning to its chaotic state that existed before God put a firmament there. It's threatening to revert to chaos. Then God stops the flood and puts the rainbow in the sky to indicate that the world will never cease by flood.

But that also is a three-story universe. The idea is that the dead are down below, and God is up above. That's why, in the Tower of Babel in the Old Testament, people are building this tower, and God's afraid that they are going to reach up to Heaven. That's why, when you go up on a mountain, you are closer to God. The whole idea is that God is up there. We are here; the dead are down there. So this is a three-story universe, and the way it works is, you are here; when you die, you go down there. When Christ returns, you go back up there; and then you live up there, because that's where God is.

I point this out because I think most of my students still believe in a three-story universe. Even though they've taken astronomy classes, they still think this way—that dead people are down there, and God is somehow up there. But, of course, the three-story universe makes no sense in the modern world, where there's no up and down. Up and down depend on where you happen to be standing at the moment, but there is no up and down in our universe. This is predicated on the idea, though, of a three-story universe. So anybody who believes in the rapture today has to account for the fact that the whole notion is predicated on a set of beliefs that nobody has anymore; and so one needs to take that into account.

This teaching of Paul also presupposes the original Christian expectation that the world was going to end in the imminent future, that the world was going to end very soon. This was of some concern to the Thessalonians.

Paul tries to explain why they don't need to be concerned because, in fact, those who have died have not lost out on the benefits of salvation. When Christ returns, they, in fact, will receive the benefits first of all. Paul, as always, then, in this letter of First Thessalonians, is trying to work out the implications of his Gospel message for the crisis at hand—the crisis of those who have died—by showing how God has fulfilled his promises in Christ, and will fulfill them further by raising people from the dead.

To sum up, Paul's letters were all written to address situations that had arisen in the churches that he was addressing. But at the heart of every letter, in one way or another, is his fundamental Gospel message: that is was through the death and resurrection of Jesus that God had restored people to a right relationship with himself.

Lecture Four
The Problem of Pseudonymity

Scope: To this point, we have examined the authentic Pauline Epistles, that is, the letters that really were written by Paul. There are a number of other letters from antiquity that *claim* to be written by Paul but were written by someone else, for example, by a later follower of Paul who was addressing problems of his own day by taking on the authority of the apostle himself. We know of such *pseudonymous* letters from as late as the 4th or 5th century. But is it possible that some of the "Pauline" letters of the New Testament were also pseudonymous?

In this lecture, we will consider the broad problem of pseudonymity (people writing forgeries) in the ancient world, then apply our findings to the Pauline letters of the New Testament to see if any of them, in fact, were written by his followers rather than by the apostle himself.

Outline

I. In the past two lectures, we have focused on the life and letters of the apostle Paul.

   A. We have seen that as an early convert to become a follower of Jesus, he developed a distinctive gospel message.

   B. And we have seen that he molded that gospel message in his letters according to the various needs and situations that had arisen in his churches.

   C. Seven of his letters survive today, all of them in the New Testament.
      1. We don't know when his letters starting being collected together into a group.
      2. Presumably, some of the communities that he addressed kept copies of multiple letters (for example, the Corinthians), although some of these were eventually lost (cf. 1 Cor. 5:9).
      3. It does appear that by the end of the 1st century, a collection of Paul's writings was already in circulation (cf. 2 Peter 3:16).

D. But letters forged in Paul's name were also in circulation from early times.

  1. Hard evidence for this can be seen in 2 Thessalonians 2:2, which speaks of a letter allegedly, but not actually, written by Paul.

  2. Some scholars think 2 Thessalonians itself was not written by Paul. If they are right, then *it* is a pseudepigraphy; if they are wrong, then the letter it refers to is. Either way, there are forged letters in Paul's name in circulation in early Christianity.

  3. There are reasons for thinking that six of the "Pauline" Epistles of the New Testament are, in fact, pseudepigraphical (that is, not actually written by Paul).

E. How can we explain the presence of forgeries among the early Christian writings? Isn't forgery a method of deception? And would highly religious, moral people engage in deception?

II. To make sense of the phenomenon of pseudepigraphy in early Christianity, we need to know something about the phenomenon more broadly in the Greco-Roman world.

  A. A number of ancient writers, such as the Roman author/physician Galen, discuss the phenomenon of literary forgery.

  B. The practice was relatively widespread in an age when it was difficult to decide who was the author of a literary work—especially given that a forger would naturally go out of his way to make his text sound like one written by the person whose name he was using.

  C. Different authors had different reasons for forging literary texts.

  1. Sometimes, for example, there was a profit motive, when libraries would pay hard cash for "original" documents from famous authors.

  2. Sometimes, especially in some philosophical schools, an author would sign a tractate not with his own name but with the name of his teacher as an act of humility.

  3. More commonly, authors would forge a document simply in order to get a hearing for their own points of view.

  4. Even though deception was involved, therefore, there were not necessarily bad motives for forging a work.

III. We know of a number of forgeries in Paul's name from the early centuries of Christianity.

    A. There is, for example, a set of letters allegedly between Paul and the most famous philosopher of his day, Seneca, who praises Paul to the hilt and indicates that even the emperor Nero was impressed with his insights.

    B. And there is a *third* letter to the Corinthians that warns against certain heresies (which, as it turns out, were from the 2nd century!).

    C. Is it possible that some of the writings in Paul's name that made it into the New Testament were also forged?

    D. Scholars have divided the Pauline corpus into three groups.
        1. There are the undisputed Pauline letters (seven altogether).
        2. There are the Deutero-Pauline Epistles, which he may well not have written (2 Thessalonians, Ephesians, and Colossians). Scholars based their debate about whether Paul actually wrote these letters on consistencies of vocabulary, writing style, and/or theological beliefs.
        3. And there are the pastoral Epistles, which he probably did not write (1 and 2 Timothy and Titus).

IV. The pastoral Epistles, in particular, appear to be later creations, written by a second- or third-generation follower of Paul.

    A. These letters are allegedly by Paul to two of his followers, Timothy and Titus, whom he has appointed to head up churches in Ephesus and Cyprus.
        1. The letters give pastoral advice about how to handle problems of internal turmoil and false teaching in their congregations.
        2. They include instructions concerning what kind of men should be appointed as leaders of the churches.

    B. But the letters appear not actually to be by Paul.
        1. The vocabulary of these letters appears to be non-Pauline.
        2. More important, the church situation that these letters presupposes does not correspond well with that in Paul's day, when there were not church hierarchies but charismatic communities run by the "spirit."

    C. It appears, then, that someone in one of Paul's churches, maybe 20 or 30 years after Paul's death, wrote some letters in his name in order to deal with problems that had arisen in his own time.

D. These letters, along with those actually by Paul, came to circulate together in the apostle's name and, eventually, were included in the New Testament.

E. This conclusion—that the pastorals are pseudonymous—is important for historical reasons: The teachings of these letters may not represent what the apostle himself taught (for example, about the role of women in the churches; see 1 Timothy 2:11–15 in contrast to Galatians 3:28).

V. In sum, the New Testament appears to contain both authentic and pseudonymous Pauline letters; knowing which is which is helpful for historians wanting to know what Paul himself taught and what was taught in his name after his death.

Essential Reading:

Bart D. Ehrman, *A Brief Introduction to the New Testament*, chapters 16–17.

Calvin Roetzel, *The Letters of Paul: Conversations in Context*.

Supplementary Reading:

J. Christiaan Beker, *The Heirs of Paul: Paul's Legacy in the New Testament and in the Church Today*.

Gerald Hawthorne and Ralph Martin, *Dictionary of Paul and His Letters*.

Questions to Consider:

1. Why do people continue to forge literary works in our own day? Are the motivations different from those of antiquity?

2. Is a forged work, in your opinion, automatically not to be trusted? Why or why not?

Lecture Four—Transcript
The Problem of Pseudonymity

In the past two lectures, we have focused on the life and letters of the apostle Paul. We've seen that as an early convert, to become a follower of Jesus he developed a distinctive Gospel message. We've seen that he molded that Gospel message in his letters according to the various needs and situations that had arisen in his churches. Seven of his letters survive today, all of them in the New Testament. We don't know when Paul's letters started being collected together into a group. Presumably, some of the communities that he addressed kept multiple copies of the letters, for example the letter to the Corinthians. Probably when Paul wrote First Corinthians, they made multiple copies for various churches spread throughout the city of Corinth, since these churches were, after all, probably meeting in houses scattered throughout the city. The idea of having church buildings where you have churches congregating on Sundays wasn't a phenomenon that took place for another two centuries. Churches were meeting in houses and different house-churches presumably would have needed copies of the various letters sent to the larger community, such as those in Corinth.

We know certainly that there were some of Paul's letters that came to be lost. We know this because Paul occasionally refers to them. In First Corinthians, chapter 5, verse 9, for example, Paul mentions "the first letter that I wrote to you;" and this is in First Corinthians, so there was another Corinthian letter that no longer survives. Local communities, then, probably collected together sets of letters that they received, and eventually these letters spread around. As travelers to one community or another would arrive and learn that there was a letter of Paul there, they may well have made a copy of that letter for their own community, and taken it back home.

It does appear that by the end of the first century, a collection of Paul's writings was already in circulation; that some, 30, 40 years after Paul had written there were collections of his letters floating around. One way that we know this is because of a passage in the final book of the New Testament to be written, which was Second Peter. Second Peter probably was not actually written by Simon Peter, the apostle of Jesus. It appears to be pseudonymous writing that probably dates to the early second century.

There is an interesting passage, though, in Second Peter, chapter 3, verse 16, where the author refers to certain groups of heretics who find the teachings of Paul's letters hard to understand, and twist their meaning as they do with the rest of the scriptures, as says the author. This is interesting, both because it shows that groups of Paul's letters were in circulation and because, in this author's opinion, Paul's letters were already being considered as scripture. When Paul wrote his letters, of course, he didn't think he was writing the Bible, any more than any other author who was writing a book thought he was writing the Bible; but at later times these books came to be understood as sacred scripture. We'll be considering that phenomenon in a later lecture.

In any event, it's clear that letters were circulating in Paul's name, and Paul's own letters were in circulation from the time that he wrote them. It's also clear that there were letters that were forged in Paul's name that were in circulation from the earliest of times. Other Christians were writing letters claiming to be Paul. There's hard evidence for this from early times.

One piece of evidence comes to us from one of the letters of the New Testament, the letter of Second Thessalonians. Second Thessalonians, chapter 2, is an interesting passage in which the author, allegedly Paul, is talking to his church in Thessalonica about the coming of Jesus. Remember that there was a prominent theme in First Thessalonians about the return of Jesus to earth in judgment. This author says, in Second Thessalonians, chapter 2, verse 1, "As to the coming of our Lord Jesus Christ and our being gathered together to him, we beg you brothers and sisters not to be quickly shaken in mind or alarmed, either by spirit, or by a word, or by letter, as though from us to the effect that the day of the Lord is already here. Let no one deceive you in any way, for that day will not come unless the rebellion comes first and the lawless one is revealed, the one destined for destruction."

This author is telling his readers that they're not to be put off by a letter, allegedly by him, indicating that the day of the Lord is coming right away. It can't come right away. First there are some things that have to happen, namely, the rebellion has to happen and the lawless one—which sounds like a reference to the antichrist perhaps—has to be revealed before the day of the Lord will come. What's interesting, for my purposes here, is that this author indicates that someone else has sent a letter in his name to the Thessalonians indicating that the end is almost here.

Second Thessalonians is one of the 13 letters that claims to be written by Paul in the New Testament. This is hard evidence that there were forgeries in Paul's name already during the time of the first century, because this letter refers to a forgery in Paul's name. The problem is that some scholars think that Second Thessalonians itself was not written by Paul, which creates an interesting ironic, situation, which nonetheless shows that there have to be Pauline forgeries. Either this letter was written by Paul and he knows that there are forgeries floating around in his name; or else this letter is a forgery, in which case there may not be another forgery in Paul's name. But in either case, either this letter or the one it refers to is a forgery, which proves that there are forgeries in Paul's name already in the first century.

One of the reasons, by the way, for scholars thinking that this letter was not actually written by Paul, even though it claims to have been, is precisely this passage that I started reading to you. According to Second Thessalonians, the end of the world is not imminent; Christ is not coming back right away. This is a message that he wants to convey to his readers because, apparently, there are Christians in Thessalonica who have quit their jobs because they expect that Jesus will be coming back any day now; so you know, why bother going to work. They sold the farm, quit the job, and they're waiting for Jesus to come back. How are they living? Well they're sponging off of others. This author is telling these people to go back to work; that the end is no imminent; it's not coming right away; other things have to happen first. There'll be signs that will transpire before the end comes.

The problem is, that's not at all what Paul says himself in First Thessalonians. In First Thessalonians the emphasis is that the end is coming right away. Paul talks about it as a thief in the night—you must be prepared; you need to be awake, because it could come at any moment, so you need to be ready for it. But not according to Second Thessalonians. There are a number of things that have to happen before the end comes. Now, it may be that Paul changed his mind, and came to think that the end wasn't going to come right away. Or, it may be in fact that Second Thessalonians is written by somebody other than Paul, who has a slightly different view of things because the end did not happen right away. Therefore he writes a letter in Paul's name indicating that it's not supposed to happen right away. In either event, it's fairly clear that Second Thessalonians shows that there were Pauline forgeries in circulation in the first century.

As I indicated in one of my previous lectures there are reasons for thinking that six of the Pauline letters of the New Testament are, in fact, *pseudepigraphical*, that is, that they are not actually written by their alleged author, in this case Paul. They are *pseudepigraphical*, writings under a false name. But how can we explain the presence of forgeries, which is what these would be; they would be forgeries, people claiming to be somebody whom they're not? How can we explain the presence of forgeries among early Christian writings? Isn't forgery a method of deception? And would highly religious, moral people engage in deception? Surely not. Or possibly so.

To make sense of the phenomenon of pseudepigraphy in early Christianity, we need to know something about the phenomenon of pseudepigraphy more broadly in the Greco Roman world. I want to spend some time in this lecture talking about the broader phenomenon of pseudepigraphy. As it turns out, we know a good deal about pseudepigraphy in the ancient world because we have authors who talk about it.

There's one particularly interesting author who talks about pseudepigraphy in the ancient world. It was a Roman author named Galen who was a physician, a very famous physician in second century Rome. Galen was an author of a large number of books, and he tells us in one of his books that one day, he was walking down the streets of Rome and he saw a book mart in which there was a book for sale that was by Galen. Two men were arguing about whether Galen had actually written the book or not, and Galen heard the argument. It turns out it was a book he hadn't written. Galen went home and he wrote a book called, *How to Recognize Books that are Written by Galen*.

It was a common phenomenon for people to forge books in other peoples' name. As it turns out the practice was relatively widespread in antiquity, much more widespread than today. It still happens today of course; people still forge documents today. The most famous instance in our memory—not in the memory of my students now, as it turns out—but in our memory, were the famous Hitler diaries. If you remember in the early 1980s they had come out. These were diaries that Hitler had kept through the Second World War, and for several days they fooled the experts into thinking they really were Hitler's diaries, until they were exposed as a fraud. Forgeries continue to happen today. They were even more common in the ancient world.

There were different reasons for authors forging texts in the ancient world. Let me give you some of the common reasons for forgeries in antiquity. Sometimes there was a profit motive. This is when, as happened on occasion, libraries would pay hard cash for original documents from famous authors. If a new library was starting up in some city, they would pay gold on the head for original treatises written by Plato or Aristotle. You'd be surprised how many original treatises of Plato or Aristotle would turn up if you were paying gold for them. So occasionally, people would forge documents in order to make some money.

Secondly sometimes forgeries happened within the philosophical schools. Schools of philosophers which typically had one philosopher, who was the head; who had a number of students who studied under him. These students who studied under the great philosopher would sometimes write treatises of their own; but they would feel compelled not to sign their own name, as if they had come up with these ideas—they were simply expanding ideas that their master had come up with. As an act of humility, sometimes these students would sign the name of their master, not in order to elevate their own worth, but in order to show that these thoughts actually are the thoughts of the master himself. Those are two reasons: profit motive and sometimes within the philosophical schools.

Most commonly, though, ancient authors forged documents simply in order to get a hearing for their own points of view. Suppose you're a philosopher that nobody had heard of. Your name is Marcus Antimones or something, and you have a philosophy that you want people to embrace. If you write a book and sign it Marcus Antimones, nobody's going to read it, they've never heard of you. But if you sign it Socrates, well then people will probably read it. People would forge documents so that their views would come to be heard. Even though deception was involved, therefore, there were not necessarily bad motives at work when forging a document. The motives could be as pure as the driven snow, nonetheless a deception is at work.

It appears that within early Christianity there were instances in which Christians, who otherwise might have been upstanding members of their religious community, forged documents. We know, in fact, that early Christians forged documents, because we have a large number of documents that are not in the New Testament that were absolutely clearly forged by their authors.

For example, just sticking with Apostle Paul, I mentioned earlier a set of letters that were allegedly written between Paul and the greatest, most famous philosopher of his day, Seneca. Seneca was a very famous man in his day and was the greatest philosopher of his time. But Seneca himself never mentions anything about the Christians; he never mentions Jesus; he never mentions Paul; he never mentions Peter; never mentions anything having to do with Christianity. Later Christians were puzzled by why this great philosopher didn't mention the great founders of the Christian faith. In the fourth century there was a Christian who forged letters between Paul and Seneca, in order to show that Paul was working at the very highest levels of philosophy in the ancient world. In these letters, they're very interesting because, Paul writes Seneca and Seneca writes back to Paul, and when Seneca writes back to Paul, he praises Paul as being a great philosopher whose thoughts are a marvel and beyond that of mere mortals. Seneca points out that he's shown these letters to the Emperor Nero, who's really impressed, and can't believe that somebody with such limited education could say such marvelous things. What's that all about? It's about showing that Paul was recognized as a great philosopher by the most famous thinker of his day.

For a second example, in the New Testament we have First and Second Corinthians—both of which I've quoted so far–and, it turns out, there's also a Third Corinthians, which is not in the New Testament. This is a letter written in the second century that warns against certain heresies. There was one particular heresy in the second century that many Christians found problematic; it was the view that Jesus was so fully divine, he was not human. This heresy is called *docetism*. It's called *docetism* from the Greek word *dokeo,* which means "to seem or to appear." The teaching was that Jesus was fully God, which means he couldn't be human, because God can't be human any more than a human can be a rock; they're different things. So how is it that Jesus seemed to be human? For docetists, it's because he only *seemed* to be human; he *appeared* to come in human flesh; but he didn't really have human flesh because he was God. This is a view called *docetism*. Third Corinthians warns against docetic teachers and stresses—it claims Paul himself as the author—Paul claims that anyone who rejects the idea that Jesus really was flesh is a heretic who is not to be listened to. Third Corinthians, then, is a letter written possibly in good faith by a later follower of Paul in the second century, when *docetism* was a prominent heresy; not during Paul's own day when *docetism* had not yet appeared.

There were forgeries, then, floating around in Paul's name as far back as Second Thessalonians. Is it possible that some of the writings in Paul's name that made it into the New Testament were also forged? I've suggested already that Second Thessalonians may be one such letter. Here let me point out that scholars have divided the Pauline corpus into three groups. First, there are the undisputed Pauline letters, the seven letters that I've mentioned already: Romans, First and Second Corinthians, Galatians, First Thessalonians, Philippians, and Philemon. Second, there are a group of three letters that are called the Deutero-Pauline Epistles, in other words, they're a secondary standing within the Pauline corpus that Paul may not have written. These are Second Thessalonians, Ephesians, and Colossians. These are letters that claim to be written by Paul, but may not have been. Scholars debate back and forth whether Paul wrote them based on the kind of vocabulary that's used in these letters; the writing style found in these letters; the theology presupposed in these letters; et cetera.

As one example, just to show you how this works with the Deutero-Pauline Epistles, I've talked a bit about First Corinthians. First Corinthians has one overarching point throughout its chapters, which is, that the end of time is yet to come and has not yet arrived. Paul expects the end of time to come when Jesus returns back from Heaven. People shouldn't think that they already have the full benefits of salvation. They don't have the full benefits of salvation. Those will come only when Christ returns from Heaven. There's a problem when people think they do already have the full benefits of salvation. If they're already leading a heavenly, spiritual existence, that can make them a bit complacent when it comes to how to live their present lives. Some Corinthians appear to have thought that they were already experiencing a resurrected existence in the here and now, and they had the full power of salvation available to them in the present. Paul is writing First Corinthians to show them that, in fact, Christ was raised from the dead, but Christians have not yet been raised from the dead. That's a future event that will happen bodily; our bodies will be raised from the dead and made immortal like Christ's body. That's the view of the end times in First Corinthians.

It's interesting when you read the book of Ephesians, also allegedly by Paul, because in Ephesians, the understanding of the end times is precisely the view that Paul opposes in First Corinthians. The author of Ephesians thinks that Christians have already been raised with Christ and "are ruling with Christ in the Heavenly places." He thinks that Christians have already enjoyed the benefit of salvation. That seems to contradict what Paul says in First Corinthians, and that's why some scholars think that Paul did write First Corinthians but did not write Ephesians.

So the first group within the Pauline corpus are the undisputed Pauline letters. Then you have the Deutero-Pauline Epistles: Second Thessalonians, Ephesians, and Colossians. Third and finally, you have the Pastoral Epistles of First and Second Timothy and Titus. The Pastoral Epistles are books that Paul evidently did not write. Most scholars are convinced that Paul did not write the Pastoral Epistles. In particular, the Pastoral Epistles of First and

Second Timothy and Titus appear to be later creations written by a second or third generation follower of Paul, because these letters differ from Paul in so many ways.

The letters are allegedly written by Paul to two of his followers, Timothy and Titus, whom he had appointed to be head of the churches in the city of Ephesus and on the island of Cyprus. These three letters give pastoral advice about how to handle problems of internal turmoil and false teachings in the congregations that are headed by Timothy and Titus. The letters include instructions concerning what kind of men should be appointed as leaders of the church, and I stress the word "men;" women were not allowed to be leaders of the church according to First and Second Timothy and Titus. Men had to be leaders of the church, and we're given instructions about how they should be leaders in the church.

When you read First and Second Timothy and Titus, if you just read them fairly quickly, they certainly sound like they're written by Paul. There are things in them that sound Pauline. First Timothy begins, "Paul, an apostle of Christ Jesus by the command of our God and Savior, and Christ Jesus our Hope, to Timothy my loyal child in the faith." It goes on to say, "I urge you, as I did when I was on way my way to Macedonia, to remain in Ephesus, so that you may instruct certain people not to teach any different doctrine." He's claiming to be Paul and it sounds kind of like Paul. The problem is that if somebody's writing a forgery, they want their letter to sound like Paul. If you read a letter that sounds like Paul, that doesn't tell you whether it's by Paul or not. Paul certainly sounds like Paul, and somebody who wants to sound like Paul probably sounds like Paul. What you want to find are things in the letter that may go against what Paul's writings were like.

As it turns out, these letters appear to be non-Pauline for a number of reasons. Some of these reasons won't make sense to you unless you can actually read the letters in the Greek. The writing style of these letters is different from the writing style of Paul. It's sort of like, if you're reading a novel by George Elliot, and then you read a novel by Mark Twain, it's clear you're really reading two very different authors. If you had a page of Mark Twain that's sort of intercalated into a stack of papers by George Elliot, anybody with any skill in literary analysis would be able to recognize, this page didn't come from George Elliot. You get a similar phenomenon with the Pastoral Epistles. They sound on the surface like Paul, but the writing style is, in fact, quite different. The vocabulary that's used in these letters is a vocabulary not found in Paul, by and large. There are a large percentage of words that occur here that don't occur in Paul's own letters. The heresies, the false teachings talked about in these letters, seem to be false teachings that came about after Paul's time. Most important, the church situation that these letters presuppose does not correspond well with the church situation in Paul's own day. These letters are about church leaders and the church leaders getting their churches in order.

In Paul's own day it appears that the churches that Paul established did not have church leaders. This might sound a little strange, but when you read Paul's letters, it becomes quite clear. Paul's churches are set up as charismatic communities. The word *charismatic* comes from a Greek word *charisma* which means "gift." Paul's churches were set up so that they would be run by the Holy Spirit through the spiritual gifts that he gave to the members of the community. Paul indicates in First Corinthians, chapter 12, that every Christian who's baptized in Christ is a given a spiritual gift. Some have the gift of teaching; some of the gift of giving; some have the gift of healing; some have the gift of speaking prophecies; some have been the gift of speaking in tongues; some are given the gift of interpreting the foreign tongue that people speak in. Everybody has a gift. The Spirit works in the community by having these gifts work together in union.

When Paul faces the problems in Corinth, problems of disunity; people taking each other to court; people coming to the Lord's table and getting drunk instead of behaving themselves; people sleeping with prostitutes; a man living with his stepmother; et cetera. With all these problems, why doesn't Paul write the leader of the church and say, get your people in order? Because there was no leader. There was nobody he could write to because the church wasn't organized as a hierarchy in which there were leaders, and people under them who were subservient to them, and people under them at a hierarchy. There wasn't a structure; these were charismatic communities.

What about First and Second Timothy and Titus? These letters presupposed church structures in which you've got bishops; you've got deacons; you've got other church leaders who are organizing the church. There are qualifications for each of these offices that are given. This is a set structure, which sounds very different from the sort of structure that you get in Paul's own time.

The conclusion that most scholars have drawn is that the Pastoral Letters are not by Paul but are pseudonymous. This is important for understanding these letters for a number of reasons. Let me give you one. There's one passage in particular that is striking in the Pastoral Epistles because it has to do with what role women should play in the churches. What role should they play? The answer is, virtually none at all. Women, according the Pastoral Epistles, are not even supposed to speak in church. First Timothy, chapter 2, verse 11, and following: "Let a woman learn in silence with full submission. I permit no woman to teach or to have authority over a man; she is to keep silent. For Adam was formed first, then Eve. And Adam was not deceived, but the woman was deceived and became a transgressor. Yet she will be saved through childbearing, provided they continue in faith and love and holiness with modesty." Women are not to exercise authority over a man because woman was made to help man. Eve was created after Adam, and Adam wasn't the one who was deceived; the man wasn't deceived, the serpent deceived the woman. Then what did the woman do? She led the man astray. What happens when a woman is a leader of the church? She gets misled by the devil and she leads the men astray. A woman is to be silent in the church and to learn in all submission. But he concedes they can be saved, nonetheless, if they bear children. In other words women are to be pregnant and barefoot.

The point is, this is not a teaching of Paul, this is a teaching of a later follower of Paul. Paul himself taught something quite different. Galatians, chapter 3, verse 28: "In Christ there is neither male nor female." In First Corinthians, Paul tells the women of Corinth that they are to continue to pray and prophesy in the church. They're to wear head coverings, but they can pray and prophesy in the church. Women could speak in Paul's churches, and when you read the letter to the Romans, it becomes quite clear that a number of women were leaders in Paul's churches. There's a woman who's named as a deacon; there are women who are named as missionaries; there are women who are named as patrons of the churches; there's one woman named Junia who is called foremost among the apostles. (Romans 16:7). In Paul's churches women had a prominent role. In the Pastoral Epistles written at a later time by somebody claiming to be Paul who wasn't, women have no role at all to play.

In sum, the New Testament appears to contain both authentic and pseudonymous Pauline letters. Knowing which is which is helpful for historians who want to know what Paul himself actually taught, and for knowing what was taught in his name after his death.

Lecture Five

The Beginnings of the Gospel Traditions

Scope: At this point in the course, we will shift our focus away from the early Epistles of the New Testament to the books that are even more familiar to most readers: the Gospels. The Gospels differ from the Epistles in numerous respects. For one thing, each Epistle was written by one author who sat down to compose a letter, but the Gospels are filled with stories about Jesus that had been in circulation for years—decades even—before they came to be written down.

In this lecture, we will consider the beginnings of the Gospel narratives in the oral traditions that were spread throughout the Mediterranean in the years after Jesus' death. Where did these traditions come from? How did they get modified in the process of their transmission? How can we know whether the traditions that came to be written down by the writers of the Gospels are historically accurate or if, instead, they had come to be altered over the years when passed on by word of mouth?

Outline

I.   To this point, we have considered some of the Epistles of the New Testament. We can now turn our attention to the New Testament Gospels.

    A. Even though the Gospels appear as the first books of the New Testament, they were not the first books to be written.

        1. As we have seen, most of Paul's letters were written in the 50s A.D.

        2. The earliest Gospel was Mark, written about a decade later, probably A.D. 65–70.

        3. Matthew and Luke were probably 10–15 years after that (A.D. 80–85), and John, about 10 years after than (A.D. 90–95).

    B. And obviously, with the Gospels, we are dealing with a different genre of literature.

        1. These are not pieces of correspondence but narratives that tell the stories of Jesus' life, ministry, death, and resurrection.

    2. They are called Gospels because they are narratives with a point: They proclaim the "good news" (the literal meaning of the word *gospel*).

    3. It would be a mistake, however, to think that, in terms of genre, they are unique writings from the ancient world; in fact, they appear very much like other ancient biographies of important men.

    4. Ancient biographies focused less on names and dates than modern ones, and they give no sense of formative influences on a person or on the psychological development of his or her character. Instead, they tend to show key events of a person's life to give a sense of what he or she was really like.

    5. One of the things that makes the New Testament Gospels unlike other religious biographies of the ancient world is that their focus is far more on the death (and resurrection) of their main character; some readers have called the Gospels "passion narratives with long introductions."

II. Even though the Gospels go under the names of Matthew, Mark, Luke, and John, they are, in fact, written anonymously.

    A. The titles in our English Bibles are later additions; they are not original to the Gospels themselves.

    B. Notice that the Gospel narratives are always written in the third person.

    C. The identity of their real authors must remain unknown.

        1. The tradition that they were written by two disciples (Matthew and John) and by two companions of the apostles (Mark and Luke) is first attested in the 2nd century.

        2. What we can say for certain about the authors is that they were all highly educated, literate, Greek-speaking Christians of (at least) the second generation.

        3. Contrast this with the apostles of Jesus, who were uneducated, lower class, illiterate, Aramaic-speaking peasants.

        4. It seems probable, then, that none of the Gospels was actually written by one of Jesus' closest followers.

        5. Where and how, then, did the writers acquire their information about Jesus?

III. Because the Gospels are not eyewitness accounts to the things Jesus said and did (they never claim to be that!), they appear to be based on oral traditions that had been in circulation about Jesus for the decades between his life and the time the Gospels were written.

   A. The one thing we know about Christianity during the 30–65 years between Jesus' death and these first accounts of his life is that it rapidly spread throughout the Mediterranean.

   B. As believers in Christ converted others to the faith, they told them stories about what Jesus had said and done.

   C. These stories were, therefore, in circulation year after year, told in different languages and in different countries from that of Jesus.

   D. What happens to stories that circulate orally for years? Obviously, they come to be changed in the retelling.
      1. It should not be thought that because the ancient Roman world was an oral culture, great care was taken to preserve stories accurately.
      2. Cultural anthropologists have shown that this concern for exactitude is a feature of written cultures; it would be a mistake to impose it onto oral cultures.
      3. Storytellers in oral cultures recognize that stories need to be modified to fit the occasion for which they are told.

   E. There is solid evidence that the stories about Jesus were modified over time, before being written in the Gospels, and that, in fact, some of the stories are not historical at all.

   F. The evidence comes in the discrepancies that one finds between the same story told by different authors.

   G. Some of the discrepancies have to do with minor details, such as: When did Peter deny Jesus? When the Jewish leader Jairus came to seek Jesus' help, had his daughter already died or not?

   H. Some discrepancies involve more important matters: Did Jesus cleanse the Temple at the beginning or end of his ministry?

   I. Some differences have an important bearing on how we understand the Gospels or how we understand Jesus' message and mission: When did Jesus die? Did Jesus ever preach about himself? Was he willing to do miracles as a sign of his identity?

IV. Eventually, the stories in circulation came to be written down.

    A. Sometimes, the Gospels are remarkably alike in their written accounts—evidently, because some of them used the same written sources.

    B. Yet they are all distinct from each other, as well.

    C. Thus, each Gospel needs to be considered on its own terms to see what its perspective on Jesus is, rather than interpreted as providing the *same* perspective as each of the other Gospels.

Essential Reading:

Richard Burridge, *What Are the Gospels? A Comparison with Greco-Roman Biography*.

Bart D. Ehrman, *A Brief Introduction to the New Testament*, chapter 4.

Supplementary Reading:

Martin Debelius, *From Tradition to Gospel*.

W. J. Ong, *Orality and Literacy*.

Questions to Consider:

1. Have you ever heard a story told about something you did that was obviously changed from the way it really happened? Is it implausible that the same thing happened with the stories about Jesus?

2. If hundreds of new converts throughout the Roman Empire are telling stories about Jesus, would there be any way to guarantee that all the stories reflected events as they actually happened?

Lecture Five—Transcript
The Beginnings of the Gospel Traditions

To this point, we have considered some of the Epistles of the New Testament. We can now turn our attention to the New Testament Gospels. As I pointed our earlier, even though the Gospels appear as the first books of the New Testament, they were not the first books to have been written. Paul's letters were written earlier, probably some time in the 50s A.D.; in other words, between 20 and 30 years after Jesus' death. The earliest Gospel was probably the Gospel of Mark, written about a decade after Paul's letters, probably around A.D. 65 or 70. The Gospels of Matthew and Luke were probably 10 or 15 years after that usually dated to A.D. 80 to 85, and the Gospel of John was probably about 10 years after that, in A.D. 90 to 95.

With the Gospels we're obviously dealing with a different a genre of literature from the Epistles of Paul. The Gospels are not pieces of correspondence, but narratives that tell the stories of Jesus' life, ministry, death, and resurrection. They're called Gospels because they are narratives with a point; they proclaim the "good news,"—the literal meaning of the word *Gospel*—the good news of Jesus' life, death, and resurrection. These books are not called histories; they are not conceptualized as objective biographies; they're understood to be proclamations of the Christian truth, the Christian Gospel. It would be a mistake, however, to think that in terms of genre, these books, these Gospels, were unique writings in the ancient world. In fact, these books, these Gospels appear in many respects to be like other ancient biographies of important men. These may not be like modern biographies, which trend toward objective, historically verifiable truth claims about their main characters.

Ancient biographies, in fact, differed from modern biographies in a large of number of respects. We know about other ancient biographies because some of them survived, probably the most famous are those written by the Greek author and philosopher and statesperson Plutarch. Plutarch's *Lives* were a collection of biographies of famous men, both Greek and Roman. By studying the lives of Plutarch and other biographies, we can get a sense for how an ancient person would understand how the ancient genre of biography was to work. It becomes quite clear when reading ancient biographies that ancient biographers were far less concerned with names and dates than modern biographers. But what is probably the most striking difference between ancient biographers and modern biographers is that in the ancient world there was no sense of formative influences on a person.

In the modern world when you read a biography, typically, you'll read something about how this person's ideas and character were formed because of influences on them from their parents, from their schooling, from their friends, in their young development. You get no sense of formative influence in ancient biographies or, on the corollary, anything about the psychological development of character. There is no psychological development of character in the ancient world because the ancient world didn't have psychology.

Instead, ancient biographies tend to show the key events of a person's life in order to give a sense of what he or she was really like. Even when a person's childhood is portrayed in ancient biographies, the childhood isn't meant to show why the person became the kind of person he/she became. The childhood is meant to show how the character of the person was manifest already as a young child; so it's quite different from modern biographies, there is no such thing as psychological development. Anybody that reads the Gospels of the New Testament and psychoanalyzes the characters within them—for example, tries to come up with a psychological explanation for why Jesus does what he does—is misguided. These authors didn't have any idea of psychological development.

One of the things that makes the New Testament Gospels different from other biographies of religious men in the ancient world, is that the focus of the Gospels is far more on the death and resurrection of their main character than is typical in ancient biographies. Some readers, in fact, have called the Gospels *passion narratives* with long introductions. Before Mel Gibson's movie came out, I had to explain to my students what the word *passion* meant in this context, since it doesn't refer to what happens in dormitories on Friday nights. Passion in this context comes from the Greek word *pascho* which means "to suffer." A passion narrative is the narrative of Jesus' suffering, and so Mel Gibson's movie is entitled *The Passion of the Christ*.

I should point out, by the way, that some of the publicity for *The Passion of the Christ* indicates that Mel Gibson's intent is simply to show what happened to Jesus during his last hours in a manner that's consistent with what the Gospels say, so it's just like the Gospels. In fact, *The Passion of the Christ* is not just like the Gospels. There are wide ranging differences between what the Gospels say about what happened to Jesus in his last hours and what's portrayed in Mel Gibson's movie. For one thing—just sort of the most obvious thing—in the Gospels of the New Testament, Jesus is crucified in about three words. The Gospel writers could have given a blow by blow account. They could have shown how long and dragged out it was, and how much pain and suffering was involved in this. There are other ancient accounts of people suffering where you do get a blow by blow account. Not the Gospel writers; they're not concerned with that. They simply say, "And he got flogged" then "he got crucified." Mel Gibson however—his film is obsessed with all of the pain and the suffering. It's not like the Gospels. The Gospels are not obsessed with that particular issue in the least.

Moreover, it's important to stress that the Gospels are passion narratives with long introductions. If you take the passion out of the context of the long introduction, then you have a very different understanding of who Jesus was. Of course in Mel Gibson's movie, the Jesus portrayed is a Jesus whose pain is our gain. The more pain, the more gain; the more gain you need, the more pain you need; and so Jesus is beaten to a bloody pulp and then gets up for more. Why? Well there are a lot of sins that need to be atoned for, and so there has to be a lot of suffering. That may be good theology or bad theology, but it is not Gospel theology. The New Testament Gospels simply don't have that perspective.

Back to the New Testament Gospels. The Gospels go under the names of Matthew, Mark, Luke, and John. They are in fact, however, written anonymously. The titles in our Gospels are later additions to the text. The titles, The Gospel According to Matthew, The Gospel According Mark, et cetera, were not original to the Gospels themselves. These books are all written anonymously. You'll note when you read the Gospels that they are all told in the third person about what they were doing—even the Gospel of Matthew, for example, which has an account of the calling of Matthew, the tax collector, to be one of Jesus' disciples. It's not narrated in the first person about what happened to me; it's narrated in the third person about what happened to him. There is no indication in Matthew's Gospel that it is being written by somebody named Matthew.

Where did these titles come from then? Well, the titles themselves are indications that the named authors were not actually the authors of these books because of the way the titles are phrased. Matthew is called, The Gospel According to Matthew. Now if Matthew wrote a Gospel, he wouldn't call it The Gospel According to Matthew. That's somebody else telling you who is responsible for the Gospel. This tradition that Matthew wrote Matthew and that John wrote The Gospel of John—in other words, two of Jesus' disciples, Matthew the tax collector, and John the beloved disciple—that they're two of the Gospel authors, comes from the second century, some decades after the Gospels were written. (As is the tradition with Mark, who was thought to be a companion of Peter; and Luke, who was known to be a companion of Paul.) In the second century, some decades after the books were written, Christians wanting to know that these books were written by apostolic authorities—written by apostles or by companions of apostles—attached the names Matthew, Mark, Luke, and John to them. In fact, we don't know the identity of the authors of these Gospels; they're written anonymously.

What we can say for certain about these authors is that all of them were highly educated, literate, Greek-speaking Christians of at least the second generation. It's an important point. They're all highly educated, they're literate, they're Greek-speaking Christians of a later generation. I stress that because Jesus' own followers were not highly educated, literate, Greek-speaking Christians.

Who were Jesus followers? According to the Gospels themselves, they were peasants from Galilee. The native language in Galilee was Aramaic. Most peasants in the ancient world simply could not afford the time or the leisure to get an education, which most meant that peasants simply spoke their native language and couldn't speak another language, let alone read another language, or let alone write another language. The best estimates indicate that in the ancient Roman world at the best of times, 10 to 15% of the population could read and write; and when I say write, I mean they could sign their names. Ten to 15%, which means 85-90% of people could not even read, let alone write their names. How many people could write a book, compose a book? Not very many people; only the upper echelons. Who were in the upper echelons? The wealthy and the elite. The followers of Jesus were not wealthy and elite. They were lower-class peasants; they were fisherman and the like, who probably never went to school, certainly could not compose books, and almost certainly did not speak Greek in the first place.

It's entirely possible that John, just to take one example, started out as a lower-class peasant fisherman in Galilee who spoke Aramaic. According to the book of Acts, chapter 4, verse 13, he was, in fact, illiterate. Suppose he started that way; now it's possible that after the resurrection he went back to school; and he learned Greek; and then he learned Greek composition, and he got pretty good at it; and at the end of his life he composed a Gospel. It's theoretically possible, but for most historians it seems somewhat unlikely.

And given the fact that John doesn't claim to be written by John, there's really no reason for thinking that Jesus' disciple John actually wrote the book. So, too, with the other Gospels. These are anonymous writings by Christians living in later decades, nearer the end of the first century.

If they were not companions of Jesus who wrote the Gospels, how and where did they get their information? How do they know the stories that they narrate about Jesus, that they write down in their Gospels? Since the Gospels appear not to be eye-witness accounts—they don't claim to be eye witness accounts, and there's nothing in them to suggest that they're eye-witness accounts of the things that Jesus said and did—they appear to be based on oral traditions that had been in circulation about Jesus for the decades between his life and the time the Gospels were written.

If the Gospels were written between A.D. 65 and 95, that means there's a time gap of between 30 and 35 years between the time of Jesus' death and the first accounts of his life—30 to 35 years. What was happening during those 30 to 35 years? There were a lot of things happening in the Roman Empire during the first century; but the thing that was most important for Christianity is that it was spreading throughout the empire, in major urban areas, as I mentioned when I talked about the apostle Paul. People were converting to become believers in Jesus. Now it's not true that early Christianity completely turned the Roman Empire on its ear. It's not true that thousands and thousands and thousands of people were converting; but dozens were; or hundreds were; and in different regions throughout the Mediterranean as missionaries would go to different places.

These missionaries, like Paul, were trying to convince people to stop worshipping their pagan gods, to worship the one God of Israel, and accept Jesus as his son who died for his sins. How could they convince people to believe in Jesus? They had to tell them stories about Jesus. Missionaries are telling stories about Jesus to convince others to believe in him. These missionaries are spread out throughout the Mediterranean, throughout the Roman world. When a missionary would convert somebody to believe in Jesus, that person then would convert their family members, and their friends, and their neighbors. When the neighbor converts, the neighbor would convert her family; her husband then would convert a business associate, who would convert his wife, who would convert her neighbor; and so it went.

Who's telling the stories about Jesus in this context of the widespread of Christianity? The vast majority of people telling the stories were not people who were there to see these stories take place; they're people who've heard the stories. Where did you hear the story? I heard it from my husband. Where did your husband hear it? He heard it from his neighbor. Where did his neighbor hear it? He heard it from his business associate. Where did he hear it? He heard it from a guy who lived across the street. Where did he hear it? He heard it from his wife. Where did hear it? She heard it from a visiting missionary. Where did the missionary hear it? He heard it from some other missionary. Virtually everybody telling these stories is telling the stories even though they hadn't been there to see these things happen; and this is taking place for decades. That's the only way we can explain the spread of Christianity throughout the Roman Empire in the 35 to 65 years between Jesus' death and the first accounts of his life.

What happens to stories when they're in broad oral circulation? The example I usually use with my students is of a game many of them played when they were younger kids sitting at a circle at a birthday party. One child tells a story to the next child—the game called "Telephone"—and it goes around the circle. One child tells the next, tells the next, tells the next; by the time it goes all the way around the circle and comes back to the first child, it's a different story. If it weren't a different story, it would be a pretty silly game to play because I just heard that story. The fact is, the story gets changed as it circles around the room.

What happens if you play the game "Telephone" not just one afternoon at a birthday party among people from the same socioeconomic class, who speak the same language at the same time? What happens if you play it for 35 to 65 years among people who live in different countries, who speak in different languages, who have different contexts and different concerns? What happens to the stories? The stories inevitably change. Sometimes the stories just change accidentally; sometimes people change the story because they want to make a point. These people who are telling the stories are telling them for a point. They're not telling them in order to give objective history lessons about what happened in first century Palestine. They're trying to convert people to believe in Jesus. Sometimes they changed the stories.

It should not be thought that because the ancient Roman world was an oral culture, therefore great care was taken to preserve these stories accurately. Sometimes that's claimed, in oral cultures everybody tells the story the same way. In point of fact, cultural anthropologists have shown that isn't how it works at all; that in oral societies there simply isn't a concern for verbatim accuracy the way you have that concern in written cultures. The reason you have that concern in written cultures is because you can check to see if there's accuracy; so the very notion that there should be accuracy came about when written cultures developed. In oral societies though, people who tell stories understand that when you tell a story, you tell it for the occasion. You tell it based on the audience that you're talking to; and what they're situation is; and what it is you want to stress. So you'll tell the same story differently, to different audiences at different times. That's how oral cultures function, and that's what probably within the storytelling tradition of early Christianity.

Storytellers modified the stories they told about Jesus based on the context within which they were telling the stories. This isn't just a theory that I happen to have, or that New Testament scholars have dreamt up. In fact, there's solid evidence that when Christians told the stories about Jesus over these 35 to 65 years and beyond, they were changing the stories. The evidence we have is the fact that we have different accounts of the same story, and we can compare these accounts with one another. When we compare these accounts with one another, we see that there are differences among them. What I want to stress is that the differences among our surviving written accounts, the differences that survive among our surviving written accounts, show that the stories were being changed, probably not just at the level of writing; but the stories were probably being changed at the oral level before anybody wrote them down.

Just so you're clear on how I'm imaging this: Jesus ministry took place probably in the 20s A.D. He dies around 30. We aren't sure which year; it might be 30; it might 33; it might 29. Scholars differ about which year; some time in there Jesus died. The first Christian writings we have are 20 years later—the writings of Paul, who hardly ever mentions stories about Jesus. The first Gospels don't come about until around the year 65 or 70. Then we have Gospels written until about the year 90. Gospels continued to be written into the second century. But all these Gospels—where are the coming from? They're not coming for notes that somebody took when Jesus gave the Sermon on the Mount. There were no notes. The stories are coming about as people told and retold the events of Jesus' life, both the things he said and the things he did. These stories are in circulation for decade after decade after decade. They get changed, and in the process, eventually somebody decides to write them down.

Why didn't they write them down earlier? We don't know. It may be that there were Christians who wrote down the accounts earlier and we don't have accounts anymore. But it may be that the earliest Christians saw no need to write down the accounts of what Jesus said and did, because they thought the end of the world was coming right away; and for whom would they be writing these things? There's not going to be a posterity who needs to know this. Probably—at least in Paul's lifetime—it probably didn't occur to people that this would be an important thing for posterity.

Eventually, though, four authors that we have in the New Testament wrote these stories down. They used some of the same sources. As I indicated earlier, Matthew and Luke had access to Mark's account, so they used Mark's account. But where did Mark get his stories? Where did Matthew and Luke get their other stories? Where did John get his stories? They got them from the oral tradition as people told and retold the stories; and as they told and retold the stories the stories got changed. The evidence is the circumstance that we have these various stories in different forms. Let me give you a number of examples.

It's commonly known from the Gospels that the disciple Peter denied Jesus three times. In one Gospel, Jesus tells Peter that Peter will deny him three times before the cock crows. In another Gospel, it's indicated that Peter will deny Jesus three times before the cock crows twice. Which is it? Is it before the cock crows or before the cock crows twice? One way to reconcile discrepancies in the Gospels is to smash the Gospels together, so you end up with one big Gospel where everything happens on multiple occasions. There was a book that was written back in the 1970's, I think, called, *The Life of Christ in Stereo*. This fellow had the idea of taking the four Gospels and putting them all together so you come up with the one big true story. What do you do about Peter's denials? Well, according to *The Life of Christ in Stereo,* Peter denied Jesus six times: three times before the cock crowed, and three times before the cock crowed twice; so that's one way to reconcile things. In fact, when you read the denials of Peter he denies Jesus to different people in different accounts. It's very hard to reconcile these accounts.

Or another simple instance—these are minor details, but they show the kinds of discrepancies you get. In the Gospel of Mark there's a Jewish leader named Jairus, who wants Jesus' help because his daughter was the verge of death. And while he is talking to Jesus, the daughter dies. And the servants of Jairus come up to him and say, don't bother the master any more; she's died already.

In another Gospel, Matthew, what happens is Jairus's daughter has already died before he comes to see Jesus, and he comes to ask him to raise her from the dead. Well, which is it? Had she died already or had she not died? The way you resolve that, by the way, if you want to smash all the Gospels together is, that Jairus actually on two different occasions came up to Jesus: one time is daughter was dying; and then another time, she died already, and he came again a second time.

You can reconcile a lot of things; but there are other things that are hard to reconcile, and other discrepancies that, in fact, are of rather important matters. For example, it's rather important that Jesus cleanses the temple in the Gospels. In Matthew, Mark, and Luke, this is virtually the last public act of Jesus. Jesus goes into the temple, overturns the tables of the money changers, drives out those who are selling animals, and proclaims that this temple is to be a house of prayer for all the nations, but you have made it a den of thieves. The leaders of the temple get upset with this action of Jesus, and so they decide that Jesus must be taken care of; and this is what leads to his death in Matthew, Mark, and Luke. It's striking, however, when you read the Gospel of John, because in the Gospel of John, Jesus cleanses the temple as the first thing that he does (it's in chapter two) three years before he dies. Which is it? It is at the beginning of his ministry or at the end of ministry, depending on which Gospel you read. And of course, if you smash them together, you say he cleansed the temple twice.

Other things cannot be reconciled very easily. When did Jesus die? That's a fairly simple question, and you would expect a simple answer. Specifically what day did Jesus die on? It's interesting that different Gospels give a precise date for Jesus' death. All of them agree that Jesus died some time during the Passover Feast.

The Passover Feast was, and is, an annual festival of the Jews that commemorates the exodus from Egypt. The children of Israel have been enslaved to the Egyptians for hundreds of years. God raises up a savior, Moses, whom he's going to use to set his people free. Moses brings 10 plagues against the Egyptians, and the tenth plague, the worst of all, is that the first born Egyptian of every household, the first born child is going to die. God tells Moses to have the children of Israel to kill a lamb that afternoon, to spread the blood on the door post on the lentil of the door of the house they're in, so that when the Angel of Death comes, he will pass over the house of the Israelites, and go to the houses without the blood, and kill the first born in those houses. It happens. They spread the blood; Angel of Death comes, kills the first born; the Pharaoh sends out the children of Israel. They escape through the exodus; they go to the Red Sea, parting the Red Sea—Charleston Heston, that whole scene—and then they escape.

Every year that was commemorated in Israel by having a special Passover meal that would commemorate the exodus. They would eat a special unleavened bread, and drink several cups of wine; they would eat bitter herbs. The day before they ate the Passover meal, they would prepare for it. They would prepare the meal. The only tricky thing I have to say is this: You need to remember that in Jewish reckoning, the day starts when it gets dark. The next day is in the evening; so the evening begins the next day. Not as with us, right after midnight; but when it gets dark. The day of preparation for the Passover is the day they prepare the Passover. That evening is the next day; they eat the meal.

In the Gospel of Mark, Jesus' disciples ask him, where do you want us to prepare the Passover? Jesus tells them. They prepare the Passover, and that night they eat the Passover meal. Afterwards Jesus goes to the Garden of Gethsemane, gets betrayed and arrested, spends the night in jail. The next morning he appears before the Roman governor Pontius Pilate, who condemns him to death; and he's put on the cross at nine o'clock in the morning on the day of Passover, after they've eaten the Passover meal. (Mark, chapter 14, verse 12; chapter 15, verse 25)

The Gospel of John also indicates that Jesus died some time around the Passover; but in John's Gospel it's different. The disciples don't ask, where do you want us to prepare the meal? They don't have a cup and the bread, as in the Gospels. They do have a last meal after which Jesus is arrested, spends the night in jail, is put on trial before Pontius Pilate the next morning. Pilate condemns him to death, and we're told exactly when it was: John, chapter 19, verse 14. This was the day of preparation for the Passover, just after noon. The day of preparation for the Passover? According to the Gospels of Matthew, Mark, and Luke, Jesus lived through that day, had a meal that night, and then got arrested. The Gospel of John has Jesus die a day before he dies in Matthew, Mark, and Luke. It's a discrepancy that can't be reconciled, because in one Gospel, he dies the day after the Passover is eaten, and in the other Gospels, he dies the day before the Passover is eaten.

There are larger differences. Did Jesus ever preach about his own identity, who he was? He doesn't in Matthew, Mark, and Luke; but that's all he preaches about in John. Is Jesus willing to do miracles to prove that what he says about himself is true? In Matthew, Mark, and Luke he refuses to do any miraculous signs of his identity, and rejects the doing of signs as a Satanic temptation. Not in the Gospel of John; in the Gospel of John he does his miracles precisely to prove who he is.

There's a wide range of discrepancies among the Gospels in details of their stories. Why are there these discrepancies? Because theses Gospels represent accounts that had been written down based on oral traditions that were in circulation year after year. These Gospel writers heard the stories, and they wrote them down the way they heard them; or they read them, and wrote them down the way they read them; or they changed them once they read them. Matthew and Luke used Mark and copied many of his stories, but changed many of the stories as well. These people were far less concerned with what we would think of as historical accuracy than with what we might call theological appropriateness. They were concerned with giving the theological message of who Jesus was based on the stories that they heard about him. It's important when studying the Gospels to study each Gospel on its own terms, to see what its own perspective is, given the fact that there are different perspectives from different Gospels, based on different oral traditions. Rather than interpreting these Gospels as all providing the same perspective, we have to see they each provide different perspectives, and study them individually for what each of their authors has to say.

Lecture Six
The Earliest Gospels

Scope: It was probably about 30 or 40 years after the death of Jesus that our earliest surviving accounts of his life were produced. These are the Gospels of the New Testament: Matthew, Mark, Luke, and John. Even though we continue to call these books by the names of these authors, the accounts themselves are completely anonymous—it was only in later times that Christians reading these books attributed authors' names to them.

In this lecture, we will consider such critical matters as when these books were written, what sources of information were available to their authors, what their overarching messages are, whether there are any discrepancies among their accounts, and whether they can be trusted as reliable historical documents.

Outline

I. We have already learned a good deal about the New Testament Gospels.

   A. They were written about 35–60 years after Jesus' life.

   B. Although they are anonymous, they were written by highly educated Greek-speaking Christians.

   C. These authors had evidently acquired their stories principally through oral traditions in circulation about Jesus after his death.

II. It is important that each Gospel be allowed to have its own say concerning who Jesus was.

   A. The discrepancies among the Gospels are important not so much for their own sake (to show that there *are* discrepancies), but because they show us that each Gospel is different.

   B. If we try to make all the Gospels say the same thing, then we are, in a sense, writing our own Gospel, unlike any of the four that happen to survive in the New Testament.

   C. The differences among the Gospels sometimes affect some of the most important and familiar stories they tell.

1. For example, the accounts of Jesus' birth in Matthew and Luke are strikingly different from each other.

2. In addition to major discrepancies in Luke's and Matthew's versions of the birth of Jesus, and his family's relocation from Bethlehem to Nazareth, there are historical problems.

3. These include the nature of the miraculous star in Matthew that leads the wise men to the exact location of Jesus' birth, and the census in Luke that required knowing where one's ancestors were from. Moreover, this census involved the entire Roman Empire, and there is no account of such a huge census anywhere except in Luke.

4. And the accounts of Jesus' death in Mark and Luke are strikingly different.

D. We are best served, then, by allowing each author to tell his story of Jesus in his own way.

III. The Gospel of Mark portrays Jesus as the suffering Son of God whom no one recognizes until the very end.

A. Even though Jesus does numerous fantastic miracles in this Gospel, no one seems to recognize his identity.

B. When Peter finally confesses Jesus to be the messiah, halfway through the Gospel, even he does not realize what this means.

C. It is not until Jesus is crucified that anyone sees that *he* is the one who must suffer and die, and that is not even one of his disciples but the centurion overseeing his crucifixion!

IV. The Gospel of Matthew portrays Jesus as the Jewish messiah sent from the Jewish God to the Jewish people in fulfillment of the Jewish Law.

A. The Jewishness of this Gospel can be seen in the opening, with the genealogy of Jesus.

B. It is also seen in the numerous instances in which the author indicates that Jesus has fulfilled Scripture.

C. Strikingly, in this Gospel, Jesus insists that his followers keep the Jewish Law—even better than the highly religious scribes and Pharisees.

V. The Gospel of Luke portrays Jesus as a Jewish prophet who comes to be rejected by his own people, so that his message is then taken to the Gentiles.

A. His account of Jesus' genealogy traces his line all the way back to Adam—the father of the entire human race (not just of the Jews).

B. The first major event in Jesus' ministry is his rejection by his own people in Nazareth.

C. For Luke, this rejection was necessary because Jesus was the true prophet and, as a prophet, he knows everything that must happen to him and is not, therefore, anxious or discomfited in the face of death.

VI. The Gospel of John portrays Jesus as the one who came from heaven to teach the truth that can bring eternal life to all who believe.

A. In John, Jesus does not preach about the coming kingdom of God but about his own identity.

B. Unlike in the synoptics, he is more than willing in this Gospel to do miracles as signs that what he says about himself is true.

C. Here, Jesus is a divine man whose words bring eternal life.

VII. Each of the four Gospels is a different account of Jesus and must be studied on its own terms to see what it has to say about the meaning of his life and death.

Essential Reading:

Bart D. Ehrman, *A Brief Introduction to the New Testament*, chapters 5–7, 9.

Robert Kysar, *John the Maverick Gospel*.

Keith Nickle, *The Synoptic Gospels: Conflict and Consensus*.

Supplementary Reading:

David Aune, *The New Testament in Its Literary Environment*.

Questions to Consider:

1. People today would never assume that two different contemporary authors mean the same thing, even if their writings were included in a single anthology. Why do you suppose the authors of the Bible are treated differently?

2. Is the portrayal of Jesus in any one of the Gospels a bit surprising to you in any way? Why or why not?

Lecture Six—Transcript
The Earliest Gospels

We've already learned a good deal about the New Testament Gospels. They were written about 35 to 60 years after Jesus' life; although they are anonymous, they were written by highly educated, Greek-speaking, Christians. These authors had evidently acquired their stories principally through oral traditions in circulation about Jesus after his death. It is important that each Gospel be allowed to have its own say concerning who Jesus was. The discrepancies among the Gospels are important, not so much for their own sake—to show that there are discrepancies—but because they show us that each Gospel is different. This is something that I have difficulty convincing my students of, because as I go through a list of discrepancies throughout the course of the semester, they become convinced that the only point of the class is that there are discrepancies.

However, the point of the discrepancies is that they show something. They show us that these Gospels are different from one another and have to be taken on their own terms. Moreover, they show us that if we want to get behind the Gospels to understand what Jesus really said and did, we cannot simply take the Gospels at face value, and smash them all together and say this is what actually happened in the life of Jesus, because there are differences among them. If the Gospel of Mark says that Jesus died the day after the Passover meal was eaten, and the Gospel of John says that he died the day before the Passover meal was eaten, it is impossible that both of them can be historically accurate. One or both of them have to be historically inaccurate; so anyone interested in knowing what Jesus really said and did has to take the discrepancies seriously. They show us that we have to apply certain historical criteria to know what Jesus actually said and did.

In this course we won't be dealing with the historical Jesus per se; we'll be dealing with the Gospels as literary products of the early Christians. But the discrepancies are nonetheless important for us because we want to know how each of these Gospels differs from the others.

I would like to begin this lecture by reinforcing this point, by talking about different accounts of Jesus' life and different ones of the Gospels to show in further depth that there are differences that one needs to take account of. I am going to do this by talking about two of the big moments in Jesus' life— his birth and the narratives about his birth, and his death and the narratives about his death—in each case taking two Gospels to show some of the similarities and dissimilarities between them.

First, the accounts of Jesus' birth. As it turns out, only two of our four Gospels of the New Testament narrate the event of Jesus' birth. Both Mark and John begin with Jesus as an adult. It is Matthew and Luke that give us the stories of Jesus' birth. Both stories agree that Jesus was born in Bethlehem even though he came from Nazareth, and both agree that his mother was a virgin when she gave birth. However, the differences between Matthew's and Luke's accounts are striking and worth noting.

For my undergraduate class, I have my students do an exercise. I have them read through the Gospel of Matthew and make a simple list. I tell them to list everything that happens in Matthew's Gospel in chapters 1 and 2, and then read Luke, chapters 1 and 2, and make a list of everything that happens in Luke, and then compare the lists. It is striking that in Matthew and Luke, even though they have broad similarities (Jesus is born in Bethlehem, but from Nazareth), their details are different from one another up and down the line. These lists ended up being radically different, and in fact, different in ways that show it is impossible to reconcile some of the differences.

In the Gospel of Matthew we are told that Jesus is born in Bethlehem, and that his father is given a revelation that Mary is a virgin, and she will conceive and bear a child. He is born in Bethlehem, and after the birth, these wise men come from the east, the wise men who are following a star, which leads them to Jerusalem and stops over Jerusalem. Therefore, they go into Jerusalem to inquire where the king of the Jews is to be born. Word gets out to King Herod that these wise men are looking for this child. He calls in the Jewish interpreters of the law, and they tell him that the king of the Jews is to be born in Bethlehem. The word gets related to the wise men. Then the star reappears magically in the sky, and they follow the star into Bethlehem. It stops over the house that Jesus is in. They go in; they worship him with gold, frankincense, and myrrh; then they leave. But they are warned in a dream not to go back through Jerusalem because Herod is out to kill the child. So they return the other way.

Herod finds out that he's been deceived and sends out the troops. They slaughter all the children two years and under in Bethlehem. But Joseph has been warned in a dream that this is to happen, and so he takes the child and his mother and they flee to Egypt. They set up shop in Egypt until King Herod dies. Then they return home, but they cannot return to Bethlehem because now Archelaus is the ruler of Judea; and so Joseph decides to relocate his family up in the north in Galilee in the village of Nazareth. That is Matthew's account. When you read Matthew's account, there are some things missing. What about the shepherds that visited Jesus when he was born? What about the census that led them from Nazareth to Bethlehem? Where are these other parts? They're in Luke; they're not in Matthew.

Luke's Gospel is quite different. According to Luke's Gospel, the entire world is to be taxed for a census for Caesar Augustus, and so everybody has to return to his ancestral home. Joseph is from the lineage of King David, who lived 1,000 years earlier; and so Joseph has to register for this tax in Bethlehem. He takes with him his betrothed, Mary. While they are in Bethlehem, birth pains suddenly come upon her, and she gives birth. Jesus is born in Bethlehem. There is no room in the inn; she gives birth outside in a grotto, or a cave, or a stable. They lay him in a manger, and then the shepherds come and visit him. The holy family then stays in Jerusalem until the rites of purification can be performed according to the Old Testament, the Torah. The woman who's given birth is ritually impure for 32 days, after which she is to perform a sacrifice in the temple, which brings purification. They perform the sacrifice; then they return to Nazareth.

It is interesting to compare the two accounts because there are different things in the different accounts. There are wise men in one; there are shepherds in the other. There are appearances of angels to Joseph in Matthew, appearances of angels to Mary in Luke. There are historical problems with both accounts. For example, the star that is leading these wise men to Jesus—how exactly is this star working? The star stops over Jerusalem and apparently disappears; then it shows up again, leads them to Bethlehem, and stops over the house. How exactly does a star stop over a house? I asked my students to go outside, look up at the stars, and tell me which house that star is standing over, so it must be some kind of miraculous star.

The funniest portrayal of this, by the way, is in Monty Python's *Life of Brian,* where the wise men are following the star, and they go in the wrong house because they aren't sure which house it's over; they go in Brian's house instead of Jesus' house, until they realize they made a mistake, and they have to go back and retrieve their gold, frankincense, and myrrh and take it to the right place. Luke's account is also problematic historically: the idea that there was a census, that the entire world had to be taxed and everybody had to return to their ancestral home. How does that work exactly? Joseph returns to Bethlehem because his ancestor from 1,000 years earlier was born there.

Let's suppose the president goes back on his campaign promises, and he decides we all need to be taxed. The way this new tax is going to work is, we're all going to return to our ancestral home, so you have to go back to where your ancestors were from 1,000 years ago to register for this tax. Where are you going to go? The other thing is, the entire empire is doing this. The entire empire is going back to register for this tax in their ancestral homes, and there's no mention of it in any author from the ancient world except for Luke? It is like this situation happening in the modern day and it not making it into the newspapers. Probably there wasn't a census. So why does Luke say there was a census? Because Luke knows that Jesus came from Nazareth, but he has to get him born in Bethlehem. How did he get born in Bethlehem? Well there was this census you see, and everybody had to return to their ancestral home. Matthew also knows that Jesus came from Nazareth, and has him born in Bethlehem, but he does it differently. There, there is not a census. In Matthew, Joseph and Mary are from Bethlehem.

When the wise men come, they have been following the star for a long time, because Herod kills every boy two years and under. If Jesus was born yesterday, they would not have to kill toddlers to make sure. They would know that a newborn is not wandering around in a yard. Jesus is in a house in Bethlehem. When they escape to Egypt, when they come back, where do they want to return? To Bethlehem. They can't return there because Archelaus is the ruler, so they relocate in Nazareth. Thus, Jesus is born in Bethlehem, but raised in Nazareth. Both Matthew and Luke agree on that, but they do it in different ways, and the ways of doing it are discrepant. If Matthew is right, that they fled to Egypt, how can Luke be right, that after 32 days they returned to Nazareth? There is no time for the flight to Egypt; since the flight would not be on a plane, they would have to walk. It would take a while. These are two different events. When people take the Gospel stories and put them together into the birth story that is told every December, what they are doing is taking Matthew, taking Luke and smashing them together into one story. To do that, you have to leave out parts of both because they cannot be reconciled.

Second example: not about Jesus' birth, but about his death. This time I will take Mark and Luke. Mark is our earliest Gospel; it tells about Jesus' death, of course, and the picture it paints is rather stark. Jesus is betrayed by one of his followers, denied by Peter, all the other followers flee, and Jesus is alone. He's put on trial before Pontius Pilate. Pilate asks him, "Are you the King of the Jews?" and all Jesus says is, "You say so." That's the only thing he says in the entire proceeding. It's as if he's in shock. He's flogged and taken out to be crucified. He doesn't say anything on the way. While being crucified, he's completely silent. Everybody mocks him. The chief priests mock him; the people passing by mock him; both robbers mock him in Mark's Gospel. At the end, Jesus hanging on the cross finally cries out, "My God, my God, why have you forsaken me?" He actually cries it in Aramaic: "*Eli, Eli, lema sabachthani?*" And then he dies. The only words he says the whole time: "Why have you forsaken me?"

Contrast that with what happens in Luke's Gospel, which is very different. Jesus is betrayed by one of his followers, he's denied by Peter. We're not told that the disciples fled in Luke, but they don't seem to be present. Jesus is condemned to death by Pontius Pilate and he carries his cross, but on the way to being crucified, he's not silent. There are some women who are weeping by the side of the road, and he tells them, "Don't weep for me. Weep for yourselves and for the fate that's to befall you and your children." While being nailed to the cross, Jesus isn't silent in Luke's Gospel. Instead, he prays: "Father, forgive them for they don't know what they're doing." While Jesus is on the cross in Luke's Gospel, he actually has an intelligent conversation with one of the robbers. One of the robbers mocks him; the other robber tells him to be quiet because Jesus has done nothing to deserve this, and he turns his head to Jesus and says, "Lord, remember me when you come into your kingdom." And Jesus replies, "Truly, I tell you, today you will be with me in paradise."

Jesus, in Luke's Gospel, knows full well what's happening, he knows why it's happening, and he knows what's going to happen once it happens. He's going to wake up in paradise with this robber beside him. Jesus is calm and in control of the situation in Luke's Gospel, even if he's not in Mark. The key factor in Luke's Gospel comes at the end, where, instead of crying out, "My God, my God, why have you forsaken me," he cries out, "Father, into your hands I commend my spirit," and he dies. This is a Jesus in control of his situation, who knows that God is on his side, and is comforted by that fact. He's not in despair; he doesn't anguish over why God has forsaken him.

What happens, though, is that people take Mark's Gospel, and they take Luke's Gospel, and they smash them together into one Gospel. Then they take Matthew, and they take John, and they put them all together, and you end up with the seven last words of the dying Jesus. The so-called seven last words of the dying Jesus are the seven last things Jesus says. He doesn't say any of these seven things in any one Gospel. There are different things that he says in different Gospels. When you put them together, what you've done is you've created your own Gospel, a Gospel that is unlike Matthew, Mark, Luke, and John. You've made your own Gospel, which is different from any of the others. These Gospels, in fact, are all different and have to be read for what their differences can tell us.

Let me give you a very brief *Reader's Digest* version of what each of these Gospels is all about. I'll go through Matthew, Mark, Luke, and John in the order in which they were written, in order to say something about what their overarching emphasis is in their unique portrayals of Jesus. Start with the Gospel of Mark. Mark is the shortest of our Gospels and was probably the first of our Gospels to be written. It's always been one of my favorite Gospels because it's a very clever composition, a very intelligent composition. Jesus shows up in Mark's Gospel as an adult. He is baptized by John. He goes into the wilderness to be tempted by the devil, and when he comes back from the wilderness, he begins proclaiming the coming of the kingdom of God. "The time has been fulfilled," says Jesus. "The kingdom of God is at hand. Repent and believe in the good news."

Jesus then begins his public ministry after his baptism by John, a ministry in which he tells parables about the kingdom of God that's coming, and in which he does miracles to show that the kingdom is almost here. These miracles are quite spectacular. He casts out demons, and when a demon comes out of somebody, the demon will cry out, "You are the son of God," and Jesus will silence him. Jesus will heal people who are sick, and frequently, when he heals somebody who is sick, he'll tell them, "Don't tell anybody what's happened."

Jesus will even raise people from the dead; I mentioned Jairus's daughter, Mark, chapter 6. Jairus's daughter is ill on the verge of death, and Jairus comes to Jesus and asks Jesus to heal her. Jesus goes to the girl, but by the time he gets there she's already dead. Jesus sends everybody out of the house except for the two parents and three of his disciples, Peter, James, and John. He goes into the room where the dead girl is lying, puts out his hand, and raises her up from the dead. He tells them, "Don't tell anybody that I've done this." Why does Jesus keep telling everybody, "Don't tell anyone"? This is a distinctive feature of the Gospel of Mark. It's sometimes called the messianic secret.

In Mark's Gospel, Jesus tells people that he heals people that he's raised from the dead, he tells the demons. He tells his own disciples, "Don't tell anyone." In fact, it's striking who knows who Jesus is in Mark's Gospel. It's striking because not very many people understand who Jesus is, that he's the son of God who has come to die for the sins of the world. Who does know that Jesus is the son of God in Mark's Gospel? Well, Mark knows it because he's writing about it. You know about it because you are reading about it. Who else though? God knows that Jesus is the son of God, because when Jesus is baptized in Mark's Gospel, God says, "You are my beloved son in whom I'm well pleased." Jesus must know it because God tells him. And the demons know it because when they're cast out they proclaim him as the son of God. No one else, though, seems to know Jesus' identity in Mark's Gospel. The disciples are ignorant of who Jesus is, and Jesus continually asks them, "Don't you understand?"

Finally, halfway through the Gospel in chapter 8, Peter confesses, "You are the messiah." And Jesus says, "Don't tell anyone." And then he says, "The son of man must go to Jerusalem, be rejected by the scribes and the elders, be executed, and on the third day rise again." Peter says, "Not you, Lord." In other words, Peter doesn't understand that Jesus is the messiah, yes, but he's a messiah who has to suffer and die. From then on in Mark's Gospel, Jesus continues to say that he has to be rejected and executed, and on every occasion, his disciples show they don't know what he's talking about. Then you get to the passion narrative, where Jesus is betrayed by one of his followers, denied by another, and abandoned by all the others. He's crucified and feels that he's abandoned by God himself. Nobody seems to have understood. Then, at the moment of the crucifixion, something significant happens.

When Jesus is crucified and cries his last cry in Mark's Gospel, we're told that the temple curtain is ripped in half—the curtain in the temple of God that separated the holy place where God dwelt from everyone else. The temple curtain is ripped so that God now has direct access to his people in the death of Jesus. Strikingly, somebody recognizes then who Jesus is. The centurion who has just crucified Jesus looks upon him and says, "Truly, this man was the son of God." The only one who understands Jesus in this Gospel is a pagan who's crucified him. No one else understands. Mark's Gospel is about the suffering son of God whom nobody recognizes; it's a very interesting account.

The Gospel of Matthew is written later than Mark's Gospel and used Mark's Gospel as a source for his own. Matthew also understands Jesus as the suffering son of God, but he goes out of his way to emphasize that Jesus is also best understood as the Jewish messiah, sent from the Jewish God to the Jewish people in fulfillment of the Jewish Law. Matthew begins his Gospel with one of those passages that students tend to hate, a genealogy—

so-and-so begat so-and-so, who begat so-and-so, who begat so-and-so—my students get upset about having to read this. I tell them, "Look, at least you're not taking an Old Testament class where if you read First Chronicles, chapters 1–9, you get nine chapters of genealogy; we're just talking 16 verses here. You can live with it." In fact, the genealogy is quite important in Matthew, because it shows that Jesus is descended through the line of King David, whose descendent is to be the messiah, through the line of Abraham, the father of the Jews.

Matthew begins with a genealogy that traces Jesus back to the father of the Jews, Abraham, to show Jesus' Jewishness. Matthew emphasizes that Jesus came in fulfillment of the Jewish Law. The events of the birth narrative transpire in order to fulfill what was spoken of by the prophet. In Matthew's Gospel, Jesus himself tells his followers that they shouldn't think he came to abolish the Law. He came to fulfill the Law. Anyone who follows him has to keep the Law; this stands in some contrast with what we've found in the Apostle Paul. Matthew's Jesus indicates that his followers have to keep the Jewish Law—have to keep it even better than the scribes and Pharisees, who are the enemies in Matthew's Gospel, who trump up charges against Jesus that lead to his crucifixion. Matthew's Gospel in some ways is the most Jewish and the most anti-Jewish Gospel. It's the most Jewish in that it emphasizes that the Jewish Law continues to be valid and enforced. It's the most anti-Jewish in that you get the most violent attacks against the Jewish leaders of Jesus' day.

The Gospel of Luke was written around the time that Matthew was written. Luke has a different portrayal. It also understands that Jesus' death was important for the salvation of the world, as does Matthew and Mark. It also understands that Jesus is the Jewish messiah, but Luke has a different emphasis. Luke understands that Jesus is the one who has come for the salvation not just of the Jews, but of the whole world. It's interesting that Luke also has a genealogy of Jesus, but instead of tracing Jesus' genealogy back to Abraham, the father of the Jews, Luke traces Jesus' genealogy back to Adam, as in Adam and Eve.

I've got an aunt who's a genealogist. She's very proud of the fact that she's traced our family line back to the Mayflower, and from the Mayflower to Adam and Eve. We're talking the first human beings here; this is a real genealogy! But why trace it back to Adam and Eve? Because Jesus isn't a savior just of the children of Abraham. He is a savior of the whole world, everyone who descends from Adam. This emphasis can be found in Luke's stress that Jesus, in fact, was a Jewish prophet who was rejected by his own Jewish people.

One of the first stories in Luke's Gospel, unlike Matthew and Mark, is that Jesus goes into his home town of Nazareth and preaches a sermon in which he indicates that he's the prophet who fulfills the prophecies of scripture. His townspeople don't believe him, and they drag him outside of town, and try and throw him off a cliff. This is indicative of what's going to happen throughout the Gospel. Jesus will indicate that he's the prophet come from God, and his own people will reject him. The person who wrote the Gospel of Luke also wrote the book of Acts in the New Testament. Acts is a continuation of the story in Luke. Just as in Luke, Jesus gets rejected by his own people. So, too, in the book of Acts, Jesus' followers get rejected by the Jewish people, and since they get rejected by the Jewish people, they take their message to the Gentiles, to the pagans, and so the apostle Paul becomes a missionary to the pagans in the book of Acts.

These two volumes, Luke and Acts, function as one big volume in which Jesus is portrayed as a true prophet who comes to be rejected by the Jewish people so that his message of salvation goes to the non-Jews. Because Jesus is a Jewish prophet in the book of Luke, he knows exactly what's going to happen to him throughout the narrative, and it's for that reason that he's not anxious or discomfited in the face of death. That's why, when I was showing you the comparison of Mark and Luke, in Luke's Gospel, Jesus is calm and controlled in the face of death. Why? Because Jesus knows that he has to die in Luke, and he knows why he has to die, and he knows what's going to happen after he dies, because he's a Jewish prophet. Luke, then, portrays Jesus as a Jewish prophet come from God, whose message, then, is to go out to the entire world.

As I indicated in a previous lecture, John stands out as unique among our four Gospels. Matthew, Mark, and Luke are synoptic Gospels, and tell many of the same stories, often in the same sequence, sometimes using the same words. John is quite different from the others. John does not have the stories of Matthew, Mark, and Luke, for the most part, until you get to the passion narrative. Once you get to the passion narrative, the stories are similar but they're told in a very different way. Throughout the Gospel, the events that are narrated are told very differently from the way they're told in Matthew, Mark, and Luke. When you read Matthew, Mark, and Luke, you never have Jesus proclaiming his own divine identity.

People don't notice this because they don't read Matthew, Mark, and Luke as if they have their own message to give, but when you read them individually you never find Jesus proclaiming himself to be divine. You do find this in the Gospel of John. As I tell my students, it's most pronounced in John, chapter 15, where Jesus says, "I am divine, you are de branches." Sorry. Jesus in the Gospel of John proclaims himself as divine on a number of occasions. The Gospel itself begins by saying, "In the beginning was the word and the word was with God and the word was God." The word was God. Who is this word that was God? "This word became flesh and it dwelt among us and we have beheld his glory, glory as of the only begotten from the Father."

The word of God that was in the beginning with God, that created the world, in some sense was God, becomes a human being, becomes flesh. That divine word that became flesh is none other than Jesus Christ. For the Gospel of John, Jesus Christ is the incarnation of God's very word. In the book of Genesis, when God creates the world, how does he create the world? By speaking a word. "And God said let there be light. And there was light." How does God create by speaking a word? In John's Gospel, the word is not just something that God spoke; it's an actual being. It's the pre-incarnate Christ, who manifests God's will in creation, and then becomes a human being to manifest his will to humans. How are you to know who God is? By observing his revelation, which is Jesus Christ himself. Therefore, Jesus, throughout the Gospel of John, makes very elevated claims for himself, far more than you find in the other Gospels.

In the Gospel of John, Jesus says, "I and the Father are one." In the Gospel of John, Jesus says, "Before Abraham was, I am." I am, by the way, is the name of God in the book of Exodus: "I am that I am," Exodus, chapter 3. Jesus' listeners know full well what he's saying; they pick up stones to stone him because they think he's committed a blasphemy by claiming himself to be God. At the end of the Gospel, when Jesus is raised from the dead, doubting Thomas sees his wounds on his hand and his side, and he falls to his knees, "My Lord and my God." Jesus, beyond doubt, in John's Gospel is portrayed as divine. Moreover, unlike the synoptics, Jesus does miracles in John's Gospel to prove that what he says about himself is true. He is the resurrection and the life, and so he raises Lazarus from the dead. He says, "I am the bread of life," and so he feeds the multitudes with a few loaves of bread. "I am the light of the world," he says, and so he gives sight to the blind as the light of the world.

Jesus is the one who comes from Heaven, who is a divine being, who proves his identity by doing signs in the Gospel of John. Jesus is the one who can bring eternal life because he's the one who's come from above, down to earth, so that people can know the truth that can make them, then, go to Heaven. Jesus, in other words, is a divine man whose words bring eternal life in the Gospel of John. This is very different from what you get in Matthew, Mark, and Luke. When you put all four of them within the same canon of scripture, however, you get all four teachings. Christian theology is based on taking the four teachings of the four Gospels, along with the teachings of Paul and the other books of the New Testament, and trying to figure out how one can make sense of them theologically, in light of one another.

My basic point in this lecture is that each of these four Gospels, however, is a different account of Jesus. These books are not all saying the same thing; they're saying different things. They have different perspectives for different audiences about Jesus. Each one needs to be studied on its own terms, to see what it has to say about the meaning of Jesus' life and death.

Lecture Seven
The Other Gospels

Scope: Whereas most people are familiar with Matthew, Mark, Luke, and John, many do not realize that there were other Gospels written by early Christians, other accounts of Jesus' words and deeds, his death and resurrection. Why were these other Gospels not included in the New Testament?

In this lecture, we will discuss these other Gospels as a group—when they were written, who were their authors, whether they contain historically reliable information—before considering a couple of the more important and earliest "other" Gospels, written not long after the books of the New Testament themselves were produced.

Outline

I. Whereas most people are familiar with Matthew, Mark, Luke, and John, many do not realize that there were other Gospels written by early Christians.

    A. These are other accounts of Jesus' words and deeds, his death and resurrection. Why were these other Gospels not included in the New Testament?

    B. In this lecture, we will discuss these other Gospels as a group—when they were written, who their authors were, and whether they contain historically reliable information.

    C. We will then consider several of the more important and earliest "other" Gospels, written not long after the books of the New Testament themselves were produced.

II. The word *gospel* has both a general and a technical sense.

    A. In its general sense, as we have seen, the word literally means "good news."

    B. Early on in Christianity, though, the word came to be used of certain kinds of books that conveyed this "good news," that is, accounts of Jesus' words and/or deeds.

C. In this technical sense, there are a number of Gospels that survive from Christian antiquity.

III. In fairly recent times, people have become aware of the fact that we have a number of non-canonical Gospels.

    A. In probably the most popular work of fiction in recent times, *The Da Vinci Code*, we are told that there were "eighty Gospels" that were "vying for a place" in the New Testament.

    B. In point of fact, we don't know how many other Gospels were written in antiquity, whether 80 or 800.

    C. What survive are about 25–30 other Gospels, many of them highly fragmentary.

    D. These date from the 2nd century and extend down through the Middle Ages and on till today, where occasionally one still finds Gospels being forged and passed off as authentic.

    E. For historians of early Christianity, the most interesting of these other Gospels are the earliest ones, which date from not long after the time when those of the New Testament were produced.

        1. Is it true, though, that these other Gospels were vying for a spot in the New Testament and that, in many instances (as also indicated in *The Da Vinci Code*), they contain more accurate historical information than the ones that made it into the New Testament?

        2. The easiest way to get a sense of the character and historical value of these non-canonical accounts of Jesus' words and deeds is by examining individual instances. Here, we will consider three of the earliest non-canonical Gospels: the Infancy Gospel of Thomas, the Gospel of Peter, and the Coptic Gospel of Thomas.

IV. The Infancy Gospel of Thomas is our first surviving account of Jesus' life as a young boy.

    A. The account begins with him as a five-year-old who likes to play and who can use his supernatural powers to have fun.

    B. But he has a mischievous streak and ends up using his power in order to hurt those who irritate him.

    C. In the end, he manages to heal all those he has injured and raise from the dead all those he has killed, becoming subservient to his parents and using his powers for the good.

    D. Even though this text is relatively ancient—coming from the early to mid-2nd century—there does not seem to be much historical information here; instead, the account has been formed by a pious, or not-so-pious, imagination about what the miracle-working Son of God must have been like as a boy.

V. The Gospel of Peter comes to us only in a fragment discovered in the 19th century in the tomb of a Christian monk.

    A. The account begins with Jesus' trial before Pilate and ends with his resurrection appearances.

    B. There are many similarities between this account and those in the New Testament Gospels, although it is difficult to determine whether this author made use of those earlier accounts or not.

    C. Most striking are the differences between this account and the others.

        1. Here, for example, it is the Jews who are *completely* at fault for the death of Jesus.

        2. And there are legendary details added, such as the robber who reviled the soldiers for mistreating Jesus and who was punished, on the cross, by not having his legs broken.

        3. There are some passages that could be taken in a "heretical" way to suggest that Christ did not really suffer.

        4. Most striking of all, there is an actual account of Jesus' emergence from the tomb, taller than a skyscraper, with the cross emerging from the tomb behind him.

    D. Here again, rather than having a historically reliable version of Jesus' life, we clearly are in the realm of later Christian imagination.

VI. Probably the most important Gospel discovered in modern times is the Coptic Gospel of Thomas, found among a cache of manuscripts in upper Egypt in 1945.

    A. This book contains 114 sayings of Jesus, many of them familiar from the New Testament Gospels, but others of them very peculiar.

B. Scholars continue to debate every aspect of this book and its sayings, some claiming that it predates our canonical Gospels, but most finding its accounts of Jesus' words to be later, possibly early 2nd century, and influenced by such Christian movements as early Gnosticism.

VII. In short, there were other Gospels available to Christians of the 2nd, 3rd, and later centuries.

    A. For the communities in which these Gospels were read, they no doubt constituted "Scripture."

    B. But few of them enjoyed the wide distribution or favor of those that eventually came to be included in the New Testament.

    C. Moreover, most of them are quite late in comparison with the canonical texts and more obviously filled with legendary accretions to the life and teachings of Jesus.

    D. As a result, the four Gospels that made it into the New Testament appear, as a rule, to be the oldest and most widely used accounts of Jesus from Christian antiquity.

Essential Reading:

Ron Cameron, *The Other Gospels: Non-Canonical Gospel Texts*.

Bart D. Ehrman, *The New Testament: A Historical Introduction to the Early Christian Writings*, chapter 12.

Supplementary Reading:

John Dominic Crossan, *Four Other Gospels: Shadows on the Contours of the Canon*.

J. K. Elliott, *The Apocryphal New Testament: A Collection of Apocryphal Christian Literature in an English Translation*.

Questions to Consider:

1. In light of what we've seen in this lecture, is there any reason to think that the Gospels of the New Testament are themselves free from later imaginary accretions instead of "pure" historical "fact"?

2. What, in your judgment, is the value of knowing about the other Gospels?

Lecture Seven—Transcript
The Other Gospels

Whereas most people are familiar with Matthew, Mark, Luke, and John, many do not realize that there are other Gospels written by early Christians. These are other accounts of Jesus' words and deeds, his death and resurrection, many of them discovered just in recent times. Why were these other Gospels not included in the New Testament? In this lecture, we will discuss these other Gospels as a group: when they were written, who their authors were, and whether they contain historically reliable information. We will then consider several of the more important and earliest other Gospels, written not long after the books of the New Testaments themselves were produced.

The word *gospel* has both a general and a technical sense. In its general sense, as we've already seen, the word *gospel* literally means "good news." It's from an Old English term, *gōdspel*, which is a translation of the Greek *euangelion*, the word which comes into English as *evangelist* and literally just simply means "good news." Early on in Christianity, though, the word *euangelion—gospel—*came to be used of certain kinds of books that conveyed this good news, that is, accounts of Jesus' words and/or deeds. In its technical sense the word *gospel* refers to one of these books that narrates the events in Jesus' life or his sayings. Some Gospels are almost completely concerned with the things Jesus did, and other Gospels contain almost exclusively his sayings, and a third kind of Gospel combines the two. Matthew, Mark, and Luke, of course, are all of this third kind, where you have both the deeds and the sayings of Jesus.

In fairly recent times, people have become aware of the fact that we have a number of non-canonical Gospels, Gospels that did not make it into the New Testament. Many people have learned about these non-canonical Gospels from works of fiction, such as Dan Brown's *The Da Vinci Code.* In *The Da Vinci Code,* the plot is based on the idea that there were these other Gospels that were in existence prior to the formation of the canon; that these other Gospels, according to *The Da Vinci Code,* were older than the Gospels of the New Testament, and more accurate than the Gospels of the New Testament, and, in fact, portrayed the truth about Jesus, in particular, his marriage to Mary Magdalene. *The Da Vinci Code* is predicated on this idea that Jesus and Mary were married, as related in the non-canonical Gospels. I should say, there are a number of mistakes in *The Da Vinci Code,* as good as it is as a book, a real page-turning murder mystery of real interest because it is witty and clever. And, of course, it contains a conspiracy plot, which everybody likes.

There are mistakes in *The Da Vinci Code*, especially mistakes pertaining to these non-canonical Gospels. For example, one of the lead characters in *The Da Vinci Code* points out that some of the lost Gospels were discovered among the Dead Sea Scrolls, which is absolutely false. There were no Gospels discovered among the Dead Sea Scrolls. The Dead Sea Scrolls are not a Christian collection of books; they are a Jewish collection of books, with nothing Christian in them whatsoever. But in any event, the idea that there were other Gospels lies behind *The Da Vinci Code*. This is one way that people have come to learn that there were in existence other Gospels. In *The Da Vinci Code*, it was claimed that there were 80 Gospels that were competing for a place in the New Testament. That is a rather funny way of putting it—as if this was a contest that was to be entered by mail, to see whose Gospel would get into the New Testament. That is not how it worked at all, as we will see in a later lecture. It's also not clear why Dan Brown indicates that there are 80 Gospels that were in existence. We don't know how many Gospels actually were in existence in the early church. We don't know if there were 80 or 800.

What we do know is that there are 25 or 30 Gospels that survive today. Many of these Gospels are highly fragmentary. We do not have entire copies of these Gospels; we have simply little fragments of them that have been discovered, for example, in trash heaps in Egypt by archeologists who were digging through, trying to find matters of interest. Some of the Gospels, though, are complete Gospels that have been discovered, some of them in recent times, some of them we have had for centuries. These other Gospels, in fact, do not predate the Gospels of the New Testament, as intimated in *The Da Vinci Code*. These other Gospels tend to date from later times. The Gospels of the New Testament, of course, were all written in the first century. The non-canonical Gospels start appearing in the 2nd century and they extend down through the Middle Ages and on until today, where, occasionally, one still finds Gospels being forged and being attempted to be passed off as authentic.

For historians of early Christianity, the most interesting of these other Gospels, from outside the New Testament, are the earliest ones, which date from not long after the time when those of the New Testament were produced. Is it true, though, that these other Gospels were vying for a spot in the New Testament, and that, in many instances, they contain more accurate historical information than the ones that did make it in? Is that a true claim, as found in *The Da Vinci Code*? The easiest way to get a sense of the character and historical value of these non-canonical Gospels— to see whether, in fact, they are historically accurate—is simply by examining individual instances. That's what we'll do in this lecture. What I have decided to do is to look at three non-canonical Gospels. These are three of our earliest Gospels; they are not earlier than the Gospels of Matthew, Mark, Luke, and John; they are, nonetheless, among the earliest of the non-canonical texts. All three probably date from some time in the second century.

The first Gospel that I want to look at is a Gospel that's called an *infancy* Gospel, the full title being the Infancy Gospel of Thomas. This book is called an infancy Gospel because it deals with a time in Jesus' life that the canonical Gospels are virtually silent about, namely, his young life. The question that is driving the Infancy Gospel of Thomas is a question that may have occurred to other people even in modern times. If Jesus was a miracle working son of God as an adult, what was he like as a kid? Well, unfortunately, we are not told in the canonical Gospels very much at all about Jesus' young life. We have accounts of his birth in Matthew and Luke, as I indicated in a previous lecture, and we have an account of Jesus as a 12-year-old boy in the Gospel of Luke—a very short account of him visiting the temple during a Passover feast, where his parents leave and actually leave him behind in Jerusalem, and then have to go back and search for him.

Those are the only stories we have about Jesus prior to his baptism by John the Baptist as a 30-year-old, in the Gospels of the New Testament. The Infancy Gospel of Thomas is one of the non-canonical Gospels that tries to fill in the gap, tries to explain what Jesus was up to as a young boy. It turns out in this the Infancy Gospel of Thomas that Jesus as a young boy had all of the power that was his as the son of God. He was still able to work miracles, he had supernatural powers, but it also turns out that he has a bit of a mischievous streak in him, and he ends up using power, sometimes in order to hurt those who irritate him, and sometimes in order to heal them. Let me just go through some of the interesting episodes that we find here in the Infancy Gospel of Thomas, which I think was probably written in the middle of the second century. It's a little bit hard to date this text because there's no reference to external events by which you can date it, but most scholars think it was written some time in the middle of the second century.

The Gospel starts out with Jesus as a five-year-old boy. In the first episode, we're told that Jesus as a five-year-old was playing by the fjord of a stream.

He gathers into a pool the waters that are rushing through the stream, and orders these waters to become pure, and they're cleansed immediately on his word. Jesus then takes some mud beside the stream and he forms 12 sparrows. Unfortunately, it was the Sabbath when he did this, and a Jewish man walks by and sees what Jesus has done. He's formed 12 sparrows out of mud. In other words, he's made something, he's done work, and you can't work on the Sabbath. The man goes off to Jesus' father, Joseph, and he reports, "Look, your child at the stream has taken mud and formed 12 sparrows. He's profaned the Sabbath." When Joseph came to the place and saw what had happened, he cried out to Jesus, "Why are you doing what's forbidden on the Sabbath?" But Jesus clapped his hands and cried to the sparrows, "Be gone," and the sparrows took flight and went off chirping. This is a brilliant scene; Jesus destroys all evidence of malfeasance. Twelve sparrows? What 12 sparrows? They have all flown off, and so he's gotten away with breaking the Sabbath law. "When the Jews saw this, they were amazed, and they went away and reported to their leaders what they had seen Jesus do." That's the first story.

Now it turns out that there's a child playing with Jesus by the pool, the son of Annas the Scribe. The son of Annas the Scribe takes a willow branch, and he scatters the water that Jesus has collected into this pool. Jesus is irritated with him; he saw what had happened and Jesus said to him (this is a five-year-old Jesus speaking), "You unrighteous, irreverent, idiot. What did the pools of water do to harm you? See now, you also will be withered like a tree, and you will never bear leaves or root or fruit." Immediately, that child was completely withered. "Jesus left and returned to Joseph's home, but the parents of the withered child carried him away, mourning his lost youth. They brought him to Joseph and began to accuse him, 'What kind of child do you have who does such things?'" This is Jesus using his supernatural powers.

Somewhat later, Jesus is going through the village, and another kid is running through the street. He runs up to Jesus, and he bangs him on his shoulder, and it irritates Jesus. Jesus turns to him and says, "You'll go no further on your way." The child falls down dead. And so it goes through this account.

At some point, the parents in the village get upset, especially with Joseph and Mary, for having a kid like this, who is out of control, and so they urge them to do something. Joseph decides, what we need to do is to give the boy an education; you know education solves all of our social problems, and so if Jesus will just get an education, he'll learn how to control his power.

Joseph decides to send him off to a teacher. This teacher knows about Jesus' reputation, so he's a little bit nervous about teaching him, but he finally agrees that he'll teach him. The teacher says to Joseph, "First I'll teach him Greek, and then I'll teach him Hebrew," so he's going to teach him how to read. First he needs to learn the alphabet, so he says, "Okay Jesus, let's learn the alphabet. Repeat after me." The teacher says, "Alpha, beta, gamma, delta, epsilon, repeat after me Jesus. Alpha, beta, gamma, delta, epsilon." Jesus doesn't say anything and his teacher gets upset. "Jesus, why don't you reply?" Jesus says to him, "You tell me the power of alpha and I'll tell you the power of beta." The teacher thinks this a smart aleck reply, smacks him upside the head, the single greatest mistake of an illustrious teaching career. Jesus withers him on the spot, and so it goes.

Finally there's another episode that happens in which Jesus is playing with a bunch of kids on top of the roof. You'd wonder why kids were still playing with Jesus at this point, but they're playing with Jesus on top of the roof. These are these flat roofs in Palestine, where you can get up on top. One of the kids trips and falls, and lands on the ground, and dies. The other children see this and they're frightened, so they scatter; but Jesus goes over to the edge of the roof, and looks down, and sees the dead boy there, just when, of course, the dead child's parents come up. They see their dead child, the child named Zenon, lying on the ground, and they see Jesus up on the roof and they think, "Ay, he's at again, he's killed another one." So they get all upset and start accusing Jesus, but this time he hasn't done anything. Jesus leaps off the roof, lands next to the dead child, and says, "Zenon, rise up, tell me. Did I throw you down?" Zenon rises from the dead and says, "No, Lord, you did not throw me down, you have raised me up."

From then on Jesus starts using his powers for the good. He heals those that he's withered; he gives sight back to those that he's blinded; he raises from the dead those who have died; and so the story goes on. It turns out that Jesus uses his powers for the good. He turns out to be remarkably handy around the carpentry shop. When Joseph is making a bed for a rich client, he mis-cuts one of the boards so it's too short. He's going to incur a financial loss because of this, so Jesus says, don't worry Dad, you get on that side of the board and hold on to it. Joseph gets on that side, Jesus gets on the other side, and pulls it out so it's the right length, thereby saving his father from losing the deal with the rich client. Well, the story of the Infancy Gospel of Thomas ends then with Jesus as a twelve-year-old boy in the temple arguing with the teachers of the Law, which is the story that we have in the Gospel of Luke, chapter 2. This, then is the Infancy Gospel of

Thomas. It's one of our earlier Gospels from outside the New Testament. Therefore, it's one of the Gospels that are relatively ancient. But I think most historians and probably everybody else would agree, there's not much historical information here.

It's not clear whether the stories told in the Infancy Gospel of Thomas are told for their pure entertainment value, or if the person who wrote this was really serious, and thought that this may have been what Jesus was like as a child. It's hard to tell whether the account is meant simply to be entertaining or if it's meant to be taken as a serious narrative; but in either event, there seems to be little here that would be of historical use to those who want to know what Jesus actually said and did. My point is that (this will be the first instance), there are Gospels outside of the New Testament, but these Gospels are not more valuable historically than the ones that are within the New Testament.

Let me turn to a second Gospel now, which deals not with Jesus' young life, but with his death, the Gospel of Peter. The Gospel of Peter comes to us only in a fragment that was discovered in a tomb of a monk in the 19th century. There was a French archeological team working out of Cairo in 1868 that was digging in a southern part of Egypt called Akhmim. Akhmim is an area that archeologists have dug in over the years, and this archeological team was digging up a cemetery in Akhmim, and they were digging up a part of the cemetery that was made in the 8th century. They dug up a tomb of a monk who'd been buried in the 8th century. This monk was buried with a book and the book had several stories in it, several accounts in it; it was an anthology of texts. One of the texts discovered in this anthology was the Gospel of Peter.

It's a fragmentary text. It begins in the middle of a sentence and it ends in the middle of a sentence, so it's not a complete Gospel the way the Infancy Gospel of Thomas is. In the Infancy Gospel of Thomas, we have the beginning, the middle, and the end. In the Gospel of Peter, we don't have the beginning and we don't have the end; we have a fragment in between. It begins in the middle of a sentence, and the sentence that it begins with says, "None of the Jews wished to wash their hands, therefore Pilate stood up." Apparently, what's happened is, Pontius Pilate has washed his hands, then he stands up, and there's a continuation of the trial scene.

This is an account that begins in the middle of the passion narrative. It begins with the trial of Jesus before Pontius Pilate. The account then continues on telling the account of the trial, Jesus' death by crucifixion, and then it gives an account of his resurrection. It begins to give an account of Jesus appearing to his disciples, but it ends in the middle of a sentence, so we have simply a fragment. It's hard to know whether this Gospel of Peter originally was just a passion narrative, or whether the Gospel of Peter was a complete narrative, like the Gospels of the New Testament that began with giving the words and deeds of Jesus, and then gave an account of his death.

The part we have, though, is extremely interesting. As I've indicated, it begins with none of the Jews wanting to wash their hands. That's an interesting point to make because the only Gospel that talked about Pilate washing his hands is in the Gospel of Matthew. In the Gospel of Matthew, Pilate washes his hands, saying that he's innocent of this man's blood, but it doesn't say anything about Jews not washing their hands. Why does it say that here? Because one of the points of this Gospel—which is different in many respects from Matthew, Mark, Luke and John in the passion narrative—one of the points in the Gospel is going to be that the Jews are particularly culpable for the death of Jesus. This Gospel blames the Jews even more than the Gospels of the New Testament do, for the death of Jesus. In fact, in this Gospel, it's the Jewish King Herod who orders Jesus' death rather than Pontius Pilate. Verse 2: "The King Herod ordered the Lord to be taken away and said to them, 'Do everything that I ordered you to do to him.'" So they take Jesus out, and they flog him, and they rough him up, and then they crucify him.

We're told something very interesting in verse 10: "They brought forward two evil-doers and crucified the Lord between them, but He was silent as if he had no pain." The reason that's interesting is because we have an account of a Gospel of Peter from the early church, we have a reference to the Gospel of Peter by a church father who mentions the Gospel of Peter and says that it came to be rejected from the canon because it had a docetic Christology. If you remember from a previous lecture, a docetic Christology indicates that Jesus didn't really have flesh and blood; he wasn't really a human; he only appeared to be human. This text could be interpreted docetically. "He was silent as if he had no pain" could be interpreted as meaning he didn't suffer, and that's why he was silent. They set him on the cross; they kill him along with the two others. One of the interesting episodes in this is that one of the robbers mocks Jesus, but one of the robbers tells the Romans that they have no business crucifying Jesus because he's done nothing wrong. The Romans are angry at this guy for reviling them, and so they refuse to break his legs. That's all the text says. They refused to break his legs, so that he would die in torment.

The idea is that when someone was crucified, the way they would die by crucifixion is they would suffocate because their body would hang down, and their lungs would extend, and they couldn't breathe any longer. The way to make it possible to breathe is, you'd push up on the nail through your ankles. If they broke your legs, you couldn't do that any longer and you would die sooner. In this Gospel, they don't break his legs, so that he takes a longer time to die as a way of punishing him, in this Gospel. We're told that throughout this Gospel, this brief fragment we have, that the Jews were glad that Jesus was being killed, and so the Jews really seem to be at fault here. The most interesting part of the Gospel, though, comes at the end. This Gospel, unlike those of the New Testament, gives an actual account of Jesus' resurrection.

In the New Testament Gospels Jesus is buried and three days later the tomb is empty, but there's no account of him actually coming out of the tomb. In the Gospel of Peter, there's a narration of the resurrection event itself, and it's very interesting. They've posted a guard at the tomb of Roman soldiers, and as they're looking, right before dawn, the skies open up and two angelic beings descend from Heaven. As they descend, the stone in front of the tomb rolls away by itself. The two angels go into the tomb, and then three people come out of the tomb. "Three men emerge from the tomb, two of them are supporting the other"—so presumably the angels are supporting Jesus, who's been crucified—"with a cross following behind them." The three of them walk out and then the cross emerges behind them. "The heads of the two reached up to the sky, but the head of the one they were leading went up above the skies. They heard a voice from the skies, 'Have you preached to those who are asleep?' And the reply came from the cross, 'Yes.'"

Very interesting account. You have a giant Jesus and a walking, talking cross. How this thing came to be excluded and lost is beyond me. Obviously this is a symbolic statement—the cross is representing the salvation that Jesus himself has brought. The question is, has Jesus' salvation reached to those who have died previous to Jesus' death. The idea behind this text is that the salvation brought by the cross of Christ brings salvation; it's salvific even for those who have died previously. "Have you preached to those who are asleep?" meaning, has the Gospel gone to those who have died, and the answer from the cross is "Yes." The narration then ends with the author identifying himself, where he indicates, "I, Simon Peter and my brother Andrew took our nets and we went off to the sea." This was after the resurrection. "With us was Levi, the son of Alphaeus whom the Lord," there it ends, it stops there. Whoever is writing this is claiming to be Peter, and the account is going to go on and give a narration, evidently, of Jesus showing up while they're out fishing—an account similar, probably, to what we have already in John, chapter 21. Here, then, we have a very interesting account of Jesus' trial, death, and resurrection. It appears that this account is no more historically reliable than those of the New Testament, but it nonetheless is an interesting account that shows us how people were thinking about Jesus' trial, death and resurrection in the second century.

We move now to the third Gospel we want to consider, a Gospel called the Coptic Gospel of Thomas. It's called the Coptic Gospel of Thomas because it's written in the ancient language Coptic, an Egyptian language. This is a Gospel that was discovered in modern times, discovered in 1945 among a cache of manuscripts in Egypt near the town of Nag Hammadi, Egypt. A collection of manuscripts discovered then, the Gospel of Thomas is the most interesting of the 45 separate documents discovered in this collection. There are actually 13 books that are all anthologies, and these books contained 45 separate accounts, including this Gospel of Thomas. The Gospel of Thomas contains 114 sayings of Jesus. Many of these sayings are unlike what we get in the New Testament Gospels, although some are like what we get in the New Testament Gospels. Scholars continue to debate the Coptic Gospel of Thomas and virtually every aspect of it, because some scholars have claimed the Gospel of Thomas was written before Matthew, Mark, Luke, and John, and is more historically accurate than Matthew, Mark, Luke, and John.

Most scholars, however, think that this is a Gospel that came about in the second century, that it may contain early sayings of Jesus, but that on the whole, the sayings that are not found in the New Testament's Gospels are not trustworthy for knowing things that Jesus himself actually taught. Some of the sayings are very much like what you get in the New Testament Gospels. For example in the Gospel of Thomas, one of the 114 sayings is the parable of the mustard seed that you get in Mark, chapter 4. Or another example, saying number 54, Jesus said, "Blessed are the poor for yours is the Kingdom of Heaven." That sounds like the New Testament Gospels. Or saying number 34, "Jesus says if a blind man leads a blind man, they both fall into a pit." The blind leading the blind, like the New Testament Gospels.

But there are other sayings, which are unlike what you get in the New Testament Gospels. For example, Jesus said, "If the flesh came into being because of spirit it's a wonder, but if spirit came into being because of the body, it's a wonder of wonders. Indeed, I'm amazed at how this great wealth has made its home in this poverty." That's a very interesting saying, but it's rather strange, and it's unlike what you get in the New Testament Gospels. Consider saying number 56, "Jesus said who ever has come to understand the world has found only a corpse. And whoever has found a corpse is superior to this world." There are a number of sayings in this Gospel of Thomas, which seem to presuppose that this world we live in, this material world, is an evil place, and that some people are trapped here. They are spirits that are trapped in this evil, material world because they are trapped in human bodies. Because of this kind of teaching, it appears to many scholars that the Gospel of Thomas is best understood as a Gnostic Gospel.

Gnosticism was a second and third century form of Christianity, in fact it was a lot of forms of Christianity, there are a lot of different kinds of religion that we call Gnosticism. They all emphasize that this world is an evil place and the spirits who are trapped in this world need to escape. They escape this world by learning the truth of their existence, of who they really are, that they in fact don't come from this world; they come from another realm; they're spirits who have been entrapped here. The Gospel of Thomas seems to presuppose this point of view: "The world is a corpse and anyone who discovers that is superior to the world." How does one escape this world? In Gnosticism, one escapes this world by receiving true *gnosis*, "true knowledge." It's interesting that the Gospel of Thomas begins by saying, "Whoever finds the interpretation of these sayings will not experience death." Salvation does not come, for this Gospel, by believing in the death and resurrection of Jesus, which isn't talked about. Salvation comes by understanding the secret teachings that Jesus delivers. This appears to be a Gnostic Gospel, designed to provide liberation for spirits who are entrapped in this world.

In short, there were other Gospels available to Christians in the second, third, and later centuries. For the communities in which these Gospels were read, these no doubt constituted scripture, but few of them enjoyed the wide distribution of the Gospels of those that eventually made it into the New Testament. Most of these other Gospels are late in comparison with the canonical texts, and more obviously filled with legendary accretions to the life and teachings of Jesus. As a result, the four Gospels that made it into the New Testament appear, as a rule, to be the oldest and most widely used accounts of Jesus from Christian antiquity.

Lecture Eight
Apocalypticism and the Apocalypse of John

Scope: Probably the most intriguing and least understood book of the New Testament is the Apocalypse of John, otherwise known as the Book of Revelation. In it is described the future course of history, in which widespread disaster and calamity strike the earth until the very end of time, when God intervenes in the affairs of the world to destroy the forces of evil and establish his perfect utopian kingdom on earth.

But is this book actually giving a description of events yet to transpire? This lecture seeks to place the Book of Revelation in its own historical context, to see how it would have made sense to readers of the first century, who were imbued with a religious perspective known as apocalypticism and who would have understood the symbolic descriptions of the Apocalypse to have applied to events transpiring in their own day.

Outline

I. Now that we have discussed the Epistles and Gospels of early Christianity, we can move to consider one other genre represented in the New Testament: the apocalypse.

II. There were numerous apocalypses written in the ancient world, even though today people are, by and large, familiar with only one of them, the Apocalypse of John (also known as the Book of Revelation).

   A. As with all genres, the apocalypse had set forms and features, which if understood, can help explain any particular book of the genre.

   B. One thing that all apocalypses have in common is that they set forth, in narrative form, an apocalyptic worldview.

   C. Thus, it is necessary to learn something about this worldview—sometimes called *apocalypticism*—if we are to make sense of a literary genre that presupposes it.

III. The worldview of apocalypticism can best be understood by tracing the history of its development in ancient Israelite thought.

A. In very early times, many Israelite thinkers subscribed to a kind of *covenantal* worldview, which claimed that God was on the side of Israel, had made a covenant with Israel, and would always protect Israel from its enemies.

B. This covenantal worldview was severely challenged by the events of history, when Israel did not appear to be protected at all.

C. There emerged a *prophetic* worldview that explained Israel's ongoing sufferings: According to the prophets, Israel suffered as a punishment for its sins; if it would return to God, he would relent, and Israel would once again thrive and prosper.

D. This prophetic worldview itself came to be severely challenged by the events of history, as some Jews realized that even after repenting, they continued to suffer and that those who were evil, on the contrary, actually prospered.

E. The apocalyptic worldview rose from the ashes of fallen prophecy. According to apocalypticists, the people of God suffer not because they are being punished for sin, but because there are powers of evil in the world who are opposed to God and his people, who are intent on destroying all those who side with God.

F. More specifically, apocalypticists subscribed to four major tenets:
   1. Dualism: They maintained that there were forces of good and evil in the world, and everyone sided with one or the other; moreover, history itself was dualistic, with this present age governed by evil powers, but the age to come to be governed by all that is good.
   2. Pessimism: Given that the forces of evil were in charge of this world, things were only going to get worse.
   3. Vindication: But at the end of this age, God would intervene to overthrow the forces of evil and bring in his good kingdom. At that time, he would raise all those who had died, and they would face judgment. The evil would be subjected to eternal punishment, but the good would be granted an eternal reward.
   4. Imminence: For Jewish apocalypticists, this coming kingdom of God was right around the corner, to arrive at any time. Therefore, people needed to prepare for it by repenting and turning to God.

IV. One way this apocalyptic worldview was conveyed was through a literary genre, the *apocalypse.*

    A. Like all literary genres, the apocalypse had certain characteristic features. In general, it was an account of visionary experiences that explained the suffering of the present age in view of heavenly realities.

    B. More specifically, apocalypses shared certain literary features:

        1. Most (not all) of them were pseudonymous, written in the name of a religious person from the past.

        2. This person is given a set of visions that usually contain some very bizarre imagery.

        3. The visions are normally explained by a heavenly angel.

        4. The visions are not meant to be taken literally but are symbolic statements about either what was happening now on earth or what would happen in the near future. The angelic explanations sometimes provided the key to interpreting the symbolism.

        5. These apocalyptic visions typically have a triumphalist ending: God will ultimately prevail!

        6. Their function, as a rule, was to encourage believers to hold and keep the faith, because their present sufferings would soon be vindicated.

V. When the Book of Revelation is read as an ancient apocalypse, its message makes considerable sense.

    A. In terms of its basic plot, John, an earthly prophet, is shown the heavenly realities about what is soon to transpire on earth: disaster, catastrophe, and rampant destruction, until the very end, when Christ returns in judgment upon evil and all those under its sway.

    B. The most important point to stress is that this was not written as a blueprint for our own future: It was written for Christians of the time.

    C. This can be seen especially in the symbolism that comes to be explained by the angelic mediator in the book.

        1. As an example: The whore of Babylon in chapter 17 refers to the political and economic exploitation the world was experiencing under the power of Rome.

  2. And the Antichrist—666—is a reference to the first anti-Christian emperor, Caesar Nero, the letters of whose name actually add up to 666.

 D. The point of the book was that those experiencing hardship and persecution at the time were to hold on just a little while longer, because God would soon intervene in history, overthrow the forces of evil, and bring his good, eternal kingdom to earth.

VI. The Book of Revelation was a book for its own time, and it should not be ripped out of its own historical context and made to speak about something that its author did not have in mind at all, our own future here at the beginning of the 21st century, some 1,900 years after it was composed.

Essential Reading:

Bart D. Ehrman, *The New Testament: A Historical Introduction to the Early Christian Writings*, chapter 28.

J. Pilch, *What Are They Saying about the Book of Revelation?*

Supplementary Reading:

Adela Yarbro Collins, *The Power of the Apocalypse.*

Christopher Rowland, *The Open Heaven: A Study of Apocalyptic in Judaism and Early Christianity.*

Questions to Consider:

1. Why do you suppose so many readers of the Book of Revelation are inclined to see in it a prediction of what is to happen in our own future?

2. How does situating Revelation in its own historical context affect your understanding of the book?

Lecture Eight—Transcript
Apocalypticism and the Apocalypse of John

Now that we have discussed the Epistles and Gospels of early Christianity, we can move on to consider one other genre represented in the New Testament—the Apocalypse. There were numerous Apocalypses written in the ancient world, even though today, people are by and large familiar with only one of them, the Apocalypse of John, also known as the Book of Revelation. The Book of Revelation is probably the most popular and least understood book of the New Testament. It has long been a favorite of Christian fundamentalists, who have seen it as a blueprint of what is happening in our own time and as a prediction of what is to happen in our near future. This is seen, for example, in that book that I mentioned in a previous lecture, *The Late Great Planet Earth,* the best selling book of the 1970s in the English language, which uses the Book of Revelation to indicate what was to transpire in the mid-1980s as a nuclear war took over the planet, destroying humanity as we know it, before Christ returns in judgment. It is seen more recently in *The Left Behind* series, a massively popular series of books written to explain what will happen when the *rapture* occurs and Jesus comes back. The question is whether this way of reading the Book of Revelation is the right way to read it. Is the Book of Revelation designed to give a blueprint for what will happen in the imminent future of our world? In this lecture, instead of taking a blueprint approach to the book—a futuristic approach to the book—we will be taking a historical approach. My argument is that the Book of Revelation needs to be understood in its own historical context, as a book written for its own time; when it is taken out of its own historical context, it is misunderstood.

One of the reasons there are so many different understandings of the Book of Revelation today—so that when you go to the bookstore, you'll find book after book explaining its prophecies, but in different ways—one of the reasons it's so widely understood differently is because it's taken out of its context and not understood as the historical book that it is. This, in fact, is one of the many Apocalypses written among Jews and Christians in the ancient world. These Apocalypses have to be understood in relationship to one another, and set within their own historical context. One thing that all Apocalypses from the ancient world have in common is that they set forth, in narrative form, a worldview that scholars have called *apocalypticism.* Both the word *apocalypse* and the word *apocalypticism* come from the Greek word *apocalypses*, which means "a revealing" or "an unveiling." The book is called The Apocalypse because it reveals secret truths from Heaven that can make sense of earthly realities. Apocalypticism is a worldview that is embodied in this kind of book, the Apocalypse; and so, we need to understand the worldview of apocalypticism if we are to make sense of the genre, the Apocalypse. The way I want to get to an understanding of the worldview of apocalypticism is by giving a brief, historical sketch of the intellectual history of ancient Israel, a kind of intellectual history of how thought progressed through ancient Israel's times, as Israelite thinkers try to reflect on the significance of the world they lived in, and God's relationship to it.

In very early times—as far back as we have records from the ancient Israelites—there was a worldview that modern scholars have described as a covenantal worldview, which claimed that the God who created this world was especially the God of Israel. It claimed that God had created this world, and chosen Israel to be his special people, and made a covenant with Israel, that if they followed his Law, he would be their God; and, as their God, he would protect and defend them whenever they were in trouble. This covenantal worldview was buttressed by the belief that God had saved the nation of Israel from its slavery in Egypt. Having been enslaved in Egypt for hundreds of years, Israel was desperate for salvation, and God raised up for them a savior, Moses, through whom he brought deliverance to the people by delivering them from their slavery in Egypt, crossing the Red Sea, and then coming into the Promised Land under Moses' successor, Joshua. Ancient Israelites who understood that God had brought about the Exodus had a view of the world that said that God will continue to protect and defend us, so long as we follow the Law that he gave to Moses. The difficulty with this covenantal worldview is that it did not match up with the events of history, because, over time, Israel, in fact, did not appear to be defended by the God of Israel. If God was all-powerful, it was, in fact, difficult to explain why Israel suffered as many setbacks as it did. For the reality was that little Israel was constantly being overrun by other nations, especially nations that were trying to establish themselves as dominant throughout the Mediterranean. How does one explain the fact that Israel is conquered by the Assyrians, by the Babylonians, by the Persians, by the Greeks—constantly being overrun by other world powers—if God, in fact, is in control?

The covenantal worldview had difficulty making sense of Israel's history, and so at one point in Israel's past, long before many of the books of the Bible were actually written—as far back, at least, as the 8th century B.C.—there developed a different worldview, a worldview that we could call the prophetic worldview, because it was a worldview embraced by the 8th-century prophets of the Old Testament. These were prophets such as Isaiah and Amos, who explained why it is that Israel continues to suffer from its enemies if God is in control. The prophetic explanation was that Israel is suffering because God is punishing Israel for its sins. God gave Israel its Law, Israel broke God's Law, and therefore, God is using other nations to punish Israel. The economic difficulties Israel had, the political difficulties it had, the military defeats that it experienced, were punishments from God. According to the prophets, if the people of Israel wanted to have their suffering come to an end, they needed to return to God. If they returned to God, then God would show them mercy, and would overcome their enemies, and reestablish Israel as a sovereign state in the land. This is the view that you find throughout the prophets of the Old Testament—Isaiah, Jeremiah, Ezekiel, Josiah, Joel, Amos—all of the prophets hold this particular worldview as to why Israel suffers. This prophetic worldview itself, though, came to be severely challenged by the events of history. Because some Jews came to realize that even when they did repent, and even when they did return to God, and even when they did follow God's Law, they continued to suffer. On the other hand, those people who were evil, who did not side with God, and who did not keep God's Law, prospered. How did you explain the fact that the righteous suffer and the evil prosper, given the prophetic point of view? The prophetic worldview, in fact, could not very well account for the ongoing suffering of the righteous.

About 200 years before the life of Jesus, there developed another worldview, a worldview that scholars have called apocalypticism. This apocalyptic worldview rose from the ashes of failed prophecy. According to apocalypticists, the people of God, the people of Israel, suffer not because they are being punished for sin, not because God is taking vengeance out upon them, but because there are powers of evil in the world who are opposed to God, and who are intent on destroying all those who side with God's people. Apocalypticists maintained that the reason people are suffering is not because of their sins; it is, in fact, because of their righteousness. According to a prophetic worldview, somebody suffers because God is doing it to him or her. You can still find this prophetic worldview in the world today when people say something like, "Why is this happening to me?" The idea being that I have done something wrong and I am being punished for it. Apocalypticists did not think that people were suffering because of punishment, however; they are suffering because there are evil forces in the world that are alienated from God and are trying to punish those who side with God. In the apocalyptic worldview, it is the people who side with God who suffer in this world. It's a very different kind of worldview that arose out of the ashes of a failed prophecy.

More specifically, apocalypticists held to four major tenets. These are four perspectives found in the apocalyptic worldview, which became very popular about 200 years before Jesus, and continued to be popular among Jews in the days of Jesus, and was popular even after the days of Jesus among Jews, and then among Christians. The four particular major tenets found among Jewish apocalypticists—first, dualism. Apocalypticists maintained that there were two fundamental components of reality. There are the forces of good and the forces of evil. God, of course, is in charge of the powers that are good. However, God has a personal enemy, the Devil, who is in charge of the forces of evil. God, then, has a personal enemy; this is the time at which Jewish thinkers started thinking about the existence of a personal adversary of God—the Devil, Satan. Prior to this, throughout much of the Hebrew Bible, you do not find any reference to the Devil at all, prior to the advent of apocalypticism. God has his supernatural powers, the angels; the Devil has his supernatural powers, the demons. God is the one who gives life; the Devil, then, is the one who gives death. God is on the side of righteousness; the Devil is on the side of sin. These are understood to be actual powers in the world. According to an apocalyptic worldview, sin is not simply something that people do wrong; it is not simply violating the Law of God. Sin, in an apocalyptic worldview, is a cosmic force that is in the world that is trying to enslave people to force them to violate God's will. Death in the apocalyptic worldview isn't something that happens simply when you cease to breathe or your brain stops working. In the apocalyptic worldview, death is an actual power in the world that's trying to ensnare you, and when it gets you, it annihilates you; it removes you from God's presence. So, apocalypticists are dualists; there are powers of good and there are powers of evil in the world, and they're fighting in this world. There's a constant battle between the forces of good and evil.

The dualism works itself out, also, in an historical scenario. History itself is divided into two segments—there's this present age, the age we live in now, which is controlled by the forces of evil; and there's an age that's coming, the age of good, in which God will overthrow the forces of evil and set up his good kingdom on earth. So, there's this age and the age to come; therefore, apocalypticists were dualistic, both in a cosmic sense and in an historical sense.

111

The second tenet of apocalypticism is pessimism. According to apocalypticists, things are not going to get better in this world; things are going to get worse. You shouldn't think that you can improve your lot in this world by increasing your technology, making scientific advances, throwing more money into the welfare system, putting more cops on the beat, or more teachers in the classroom—you can't improve your lot in this world because things are going to get worse. They're going to get worse because this age is controlled by the powers of evil, and they're going to continue asserting their power until the end of this age when, literally, all Hell is going to break out.

The third tenet of apocalypticism is vindication. At the end of this age, God will intervene to overthrow the forces of evil and bring in his good kingdom. The end of this age will be a terrible time of suffering, but God will vindicate himself, and his creation, and his name. At that time, when God brings in his good kingdom, he will destroy the forces of evil. The Devil will be destroyed, the demons will be destroyed, and all suffering will be taken out of the world. He'll bring in his good kingdom and there will be a resurrection of the dead. People side with either the forces of good or the forces of evil—everybody is on one side or the other—but nobody should think that they can side with the forces of evil, prosper in this world, rise to the top of the heap, and then die and get away with it. They can't get away with it because at the end, God is going to raise people from the dead, and those who have sided with evil will face judgment, eternal torment; whereas those who have sided with God, and have suffered in this world as a result, will be raised and be given an eternal reward. There'll be a resurrection of the dead at the end of this age with the righteous inheriting the Kingdom of God.

When, though, is this going to happen? When will the end come? Apocalypticists believed they were living at the end of time—the end was very near, it was right around the corner. The reason for thinking this was to encourage people that, if they're suffering now, if they'll hold on for just a little while longer, God will intervene, overthrow the forces of evil, and reward his own righteous. How near is this end? "Truly, I tell you, there are some standing here who will not taste death before they see that the Kingdom of God has come in power," the words of Jesus, Mark, chapter 9, verse 1. "Truly, I tell you," says Jesus, "this generation will not pass away before all these things take place"—Mark, chapter 13, verse 30.

Jesus of Nazareth himself appears to have been an apocalypticist, who believed in a dualistic worldview, where there are forces of good and forces of evil, who believed in opposing the forces of evil because the end was near, soon to come. Jesus' followers were also apocalypticists, who believed that the end was coming soon. We've also already seen a hint of this in the writings of the apostle Paul, who, like Jesus before him, was an apocalypticist, who thought that the end was coming soon, who thought that Jesus would soon return. Paul wasn't the only one. The author of the Book of Revelation was also an apocalypticist who embodied his apocalyptic worldview in a work that we now call an Apocalypse.

The Apocalypse is a genre of literature that embodies an apocalyptic worldview. People today aren't used to reading this genre of literature, so when they read the Book of Revelation, it sounds completely unlike anything they've read before. Well, it's simply because they haven't read ancient literature enough. If you read enough ancient literature, you run across Apocalypses, written both by Jews and by Christians, and you realize it was a form of writing, a kind of writing. Just as today people write novels, and short stories, and limerick poems, in the ancient world, people wrote Apocalypses.

To understand this one Apocalypse, then, we have to understand how the genre of the Apocalypse worked. Let me say something about the literary features common in Apocalypses in the ancient world. Most Apocalypses in the ancient world were *pseudonymous*, meaning they were written under a false name. Usually, a person would write in the name of a famous religious person in the past, so we have Apocalypses written by Abraham, allegedly, and Enoch. We even have an Apocalypse allegedly written by Adam of Adam-and-Eve fame. Why write in the name of a famous person from the past? Because to whom else would God reveal his secrets of the future of the world, but to one of his famous religious ones, his famous righteous ones. So, these books are written pseudonymously.

Second, this person is a prophet who is given a set of visions that usually contain some very bizarre imagery. The very strange imagery of the Book of Revelation is not unusual in Apocalypses; most Apocalypses contain visions that reveal very bizarre imagery. These visions are normally explained by some heavenly being to the prophet, so that the prophet can understand what is being revealed to him. The visions are not meant to be taken literally; they are symbolic statements, either about what's happening now on earth, or about what will happen in the near future. The angelic explanations sometimes provide a key to interpreting the symbolism of the visions. These apocalyptic visions in the Apocalypses typically have a triumphalist ending, showing that God will ultimately prevail. Their function, as a rule, is to encourage believers to hold on and to keep the faith because their present sufferings will soon be vindicated. There are a number of Apocalypses from the ancient world that have these literary features and the Book of Revelation is one of them.

When the Book of Revelation is read as an ancient Apocalypse—in other words, when it's put in its own historical, literary context—then its message makes considerable sense. The way the basic plot of the Book of Revelation goes is as follows. There's a prophet named John who has been exiled on to the island of Patmos who is given a vision. In this vision, he sees one like a son of a man, who is representative of Jesus himself, who tells him that he's going to reveal to him the nature of heavenly realities, so that he can understand what's happening on earth. The prophet John then looks up in the sky and he sees a window in Heaven—remember, these people are working with a three-storied universe, so that up in Heaven, up above, is where God is. He sees a window in the Heaven, and then he shoots up through this window, and he enters into the Heavenly places, and he sees the throne of God with God on the throne. Beside the throne is a lamb, a lamb as if slain. On the throne, the one sitting on the throne is holding a scroll that is sealed with seven seals. These seals have to be broken before the scroll can be opened. The scroll records the future of the earth, but no one is worthy to break the scrolls; no one is of sufficient dignity to break the scrolls except for the lamb.

The lamb received the scroll—the lamb, of course, is a representation of Christ, the one who was slain for the sins of the world—the lamb takes the scroll and starts breaking the seals. As he breaks each seal on the scroll, a disaster hits the earth—war, disease, famine, destruction—with the breaking of every seal, a new calamity hits. When he breaks the seventh seal, though, instead of another calamity, what happens is, we're introduced to seven angels who have seven trumpets and they blow their trumpets one at a time, and as each one blows the trumpet, another disaster hits the earth. When the seventh trumpet is blown, however, instead of another disaster, we're introduced to seven angels who have seven huge bowls of God's wrath, and they pour out God's wrath upon the earth, one at a time. Seven seals, followed by seven trumpets, followed by seven bowls of God's wrath, each of them showing calamity hitting the earth. These are the end times when things get worse and worse on earth until the end massive destruction. But then at the end, God intervenes himself, and God sends Christ from Heaven. He sends Christ on a white horse to do battle with the anti-Christ, his opponent on earth. Christ wins the battle gloriously, and then we have the beginning of a millennial age, a utopian world of 1,000 years in which righteousness reigns on the earth, after which there's a resurrection of the dead and God then creates a new Heaven and a new earth, where there'll be no more sin; there'll be no more suffering; there'll be no more war; there'll be no more hunger; there'll be no more disease; there'll be no more loneliness; there'll be no more pain of any kind; there'll only be good, as God rules the earth in his righteousness, so that the righteous followers of God are given an eternal reward. This, then, is the Book of Revelation.

The mistake is to take this book and its imagery as referring to things that are yet to happen in our own world. In fact, the symbolism of the Book of Revelation—as it is explained to John, the prophet, by the angelic mediator—the symbolism is clearly referring to events transpiring in John's own day. This is a book that is written in the 1st century, probably at the end of the 1st century, maybe around the year 90 or 95, and it's written to deal with events that had transpired in the 1st century. It's giving a symbolic vision of how this prophet is understanding his own world, not the world to come in our own future. Let me give you an example of how this works, of how the symbolism works, by actually giving two examples to show that this book is best understood as, in fact, referring to events transpiring in the prophet's own day.

The first passage that I want to look at has to do with the famous whore of Babylon from chapter 17. One of the seven angels who had one of the seven bowls of God's wrath appears to the prophet John and he says in chapter 17, verse 1, "Come, I will show you the judgment of the great whore who is seated on many waters, with whom the kings of the earth committed fornication, and with the wine of whose fornication the inhabitants of the earth have become drunk." Okay, so there's a whore and the kings of the earth have committed fornication with this whore. And so he's taken out into the wilderness in spirit, and the prophet sees a woman seated on a scarlet beast that was full of blasphemous names, and this beast had seven heads and ten horns. The woman is clothed in purple and scarlet, she's adorned with gold and jewels and pearls, and she holds in her hand a cup full of abominations and the impurities of her fornication. This is a very strange vision. On her head is written a name, a mystery; the name is Babylon the Great Mother of Whores and of Earth's Abominations. "And I saw that the woman was drunk with the blood of the saints and the blood of the witnesses of Jesus." What in the world is this? Is this something that's yet to happen in our own future? The angel indicates who this whore is, and anybody who understands about the 1st century knows quite clearly whom this whore represents. The angel says, "This calls for a mind that has wisdom: the seven heads [of the beast] on which the whore is seated are seven mountains. ... The ten horns are ten kings that have not yet received a kingdom, but are to receive authority as kings for one hour together with the beast. They are united in yielding their power and authority to the beast."

He goes on to explain at the end who the woman is. It's a woman who's seated on the beast with seven heads; the seven heads represent seven mountains. "The woman you saw is the great city that rules over the kings of the earth." The whore of Babylon represents a city seated on seven hills—what is the city built on seven hills? As any student of antiquity knows, that's the city of Rome. Rome, the city built on seven hills; Rome, the city that had conquered the world; Rome, the city to which the kings of the earth were subservient; Rome, the city that had persecuted the Christians. This is a vision not of our own future; it's a vision of Rome in the time of the prophet, who's understood to be a whore that has committed abominations with the other nations of the earth and has persecuted the Christians. Rome is understood to be a whore that is going to be dethroned from her seat, who's going to be destroyed when God intervenes for his name, and sets up his good kingdom on earth.

I'll give you a second example of how this book is referring to events of its own day. Revelation, chapter 13, is the famous passage of the rise of the anti-Christ, who is a beast that rises out of the sea with ten horns and seven heads—that sounds familiar, that's where you get that 17, so you think, well this beast is Rome again. In fact, this beast is the anti-Christ; it blasphemes against God, and it makes war on the saints and conquers them. Then we're told an interesting passage, the number of the beast: "Let anyone understand who can read the number of the beast is the number of a person, its number is 666." The number of the beast—what is this referring to? People have written all sorts of books trying to argue whom 666 refers to. When I was in college, there was a book written to try to show that the pope was 666 and another book was written to try show that Henry Kissinger was 666—there are all sorts of theories. Let me tell you the theory that most biblical scholars hold to.

Parts of the Book of Revelation were written over a long period of time. The emperor of Rome who first persecuted the Christians was the Emperor Nero. When you spell the name Caesar Nero in Hebrew letters, each Hebrew letter has a numerical equivalent; *aleph* equals one, *beth* equals two, etc. When you add up the letters of the name Caesar Nero, it adds up to 666. It's interesting that in some manuscripts of the Book of Revelation, instead of saying the number of the beast is 666, some manuscripts say the number of the best is 616. You can spell Caesar Nero's name two ways; one way with a final *nun* on the end of Nero, one without. Without the final *nun*, the name Nero adds up to 616. This author is not talking about somebody in our future—he's talking about Rome and its emperors. The anti-Christ, the opponent of Christ, was the Emperor Nero. The point of the Book of Revelation is that people that were reading it, its audience, were experiencing hardship and persecution, and this book is telling them that they need to hold on a little while longer because God is soon going to intervene in history, to overthrow the forces of evil as represented by the Roman Empire, and bring His good eternal kingdom to earth.

In sum, the Book of Revelation was a book for its own time, and it should not be ripped out of its own historical context and made to speak about something that its author did not have in mind at all—our own future here at the beginning of the 21st century, some 1,900 years after the book itself was composed.

Lecture Nine
The Copyists Who Gave Us Scripture

Scope: In the previous lecture, we saw how the early Christian writings, including those of the New Testament, were circulated, but *why* were they circulated? What about these books made Christians eager to read and study them?

As we will see in this lecture, one of the things that made Christianity novel in the ancient world is that it was a religion largely based on books (this wasn't true of other Roman religions). Books were important because Christianity developed into a religion based on *authority*—originally the authority of Jesus, then of his apostles. But when the apostles were no longer living, what could serve as the authoritative basis of the faith? It was the books the apostles left behind. However, there were numerous books that *claimed* to be written by apostles but weren't (the pseudepigrapha). The decision about which books to accept as authoritative was a decision that had profound effects on the beliefs and practices of the early Christians.

Outline

I. Now that we have looked at some of the more important writings of the New Testament—Gospels, Epistles, and the apocalypse—we can take a step back and ask how these writings actually came down to us today.

   A. We need always to remember that in the ancient world, the production and dissemination of books was quite different from today.
      1. There were no printing presses, photocopy machines, or electronic transfers of information.
      2. For books to be distributed, they had to be reproduced, and they could be reproduced only by hand, one word, one letter, at a time.
      3. Not only was this a slow and painstaking process that disallowed the mass production of books in the modern sense, but it was also a process prone to errors.

4. Anyone copying a book out by longhand will make mistakes; those who wish to see can try it for themselves!

5. This means that in the ancient world, when there was more than one copy of a book, there was no guarantee that the multiple copies would be alike in all their details; odds were that they would, in fact, be different from one another.

B. We do not have the originals of any of the letters of Paul, the Gospels, or the apocalypse—indeed, of any early Christian text.

1. What we have are copies, the vast majority of them produced centuries after the originals from copies that were also centuries removed from the originals and that had themselves been made from earlier copies.

2. Dating back to AD 125-140, the earliest manuscript in existence is written on papyrus in codex form (like a book); it is called P52 because it is the 52nd papyrus that has been catalogued.

3. Starting in the 4th century, scribes copied documents on to parchment.

4. We don't have complete books of the New Testament on any surviving manuscripts until about the end of the 3rd century.

5. We don't have complete copies of the New Testament until the 4th century, 300 years after the books themselves were written.

6. Of the thousands of copies of the New Testament that now survive, most date from the Middles Ages, and no two are exactly alike in all their wording (with the exception of the smallest surviving fragments).

C. Scribes who copied the Christian texts obviously changed them. This leads to a host of interesting questions that we will address in this lecture.

1. Why were the originals of the New Testament changed in copying?

2. How extensive are the changes?

3. How many copies do we now have?

4. If all of them contain mistakes, are there places where we don't know what the authors originally wrote?

II. The fact that the originals do not survive was occasionally noted during antiquity and the Middle Ages, but it was not until relatively modern times that it was recognized as a major problem.

   A. On occasion, early Christian authors commenting on the text of Scripture will point out that different manuscripts have different texts in some places.

   B. And scribes in the Middle Ages would sometimes correct a manuscript they were copying from some other manuscript.

   C. But it was not until after the invention of the printing press—when printers had to decide which form of the text to set up in type— that the vast differences among our manuscripts came to be recognized.

   D. A major breakthrough occurred in 1707, with the publication of an edition of the Greek New Testament by Oxford scholar John Mill.

      1. Mill had spent 30 years of his life comparing the Greek manuscripts of the New Testament available to him and considering the ancient translations of the New Testament into other languages and the quotations of the New Testament by the early church fathers.

      2. He compiled all his results and published an edition of the New Testament that included an "apparatus" of variant readings he had discovered, that is, places where there were significant differences among the manuscripts.

      3. To the shock and dismay of many of his contemporaries, Mill's apparatus indicated 30,000 places of variation. And these were only the variant readings he considered "significant" (others that he knew about, he didn't include)!

   E. Since then, scholars have uncovered many more variant readings among our manuscripts.

      1. Mill had examined 100 manuscripts. Today, we have well over 5000 manuscripts available.

      2. As a result, we don't actually know how many variant readings survive; no one has been able to count them all.

      3. Perhaps it is easiest to put the number in comparative terms. We know of more variants in our manuscripts than there are words in the New Testament.

III. There are a variety of ways to describe the differences among our manuscripts.

    A. Some variants appear to have been made by accident; others, intentionally (by scribes wanting to modify the texts).

        1. Accidental changes would include such relatively innocent differences as changes in spelling, the omission of a word or line, or the accidental rearrangement of words.

        2. Intentional changes would include places where scribes modified the text because they thought it contained an error or a reading that was problematic.

    B. Some of these variants—especially the intentional ones—are significant for understanding the meaning of the text.

        1. Was the story of Jesus and the adulteress in John 8 originally found in the Fourth Gospel, or was it added later?

        2. Were the last 12 verses of Mark, where Jesus appears to his disciples after his resurrection, original or added later?

        3. Did Jesus pray for his executioners to be forgiven "for they don't know what they are doing," as found in some manuscripts of Luke but not in others?

        4. When Jesus was approached by a leper to be healed in Mark 1, did he feel compassion for the man or did he get angry?

IV. Given the variety of our manuscripts and the mass of scribal changes in them, scholars have had to devise ways of determining what the original text was wherever there is variation.

    A. Some of the criteria textual critics use involve the character of the manuscripts supporting one reading over another: Which reading do the oldest manuscripts have? Which reading is found more broadly throughout the tradition? Which reading is found in our "best" manuscripts?

    B. Other criteria involve the nature of the individual readings themselves: Which readings are more in line with the writing style, vocabulary, and theology of the author otherwise? Which ones would have been more likely seen to be "better" to a scribe? (The reading that is more difficult is usually through to be the one that is original, because scribes are more likely to have tried to resolve a problematic statement than to create one.)

    C. Using these criteria, we can, in most instances, be reasonably sure that we know what the authors originally wrote. But there will always be places where we are not sure.

V. It is important to remember when we read the New Testament that we are not reading the originals as produced by the ancient authors. We are reading translations into English of Greek texts whose originals do not survive; these translations are based on copies of the originals, and all of these copies have errors in them. In some places, we may not even know what an author originally said.

Essential Reading:

Bart D. Ehrman, *Misquoting Jesus: The Story Behind Who Changed the Bible and Why.*

————, *The New Testament: A Historical Introduction to the Early Christian Writings*, chapter 29.

Supplementary Reading:

Bruce M. Metzger and Bart D. Ehrman, *The Text of the New Testament: Its Transmission, Corruption, and Restoration.*

David Parker, *The Living Text of the Gospels.*

Questions to Consider:

1. In your opinion, is the "authority" of the New Testament affected by the circumstance that we don't have the originals and, in some places, may not know what the original authors actually wrote?

2. Why do you suppose the early Christians did not bother to preserve the original texts of the New Testament writings?

Lecture Nine—Transcript
The Copyists Who Gave Us Scripture

Now that we've looked at some of the more important writings of the New Testament—Gospels, Epistles, and the Apocalypse—we can take a step back and ask how these writings actually came down to us today.

We need always to remember that in the ancient world, the production and dissemination of books was quite different from today. There were no printing presses, photocopy machines, or electronic transfers of information. For books to be distributed, they had to be reproduced, and they could be reproduced only by hand, one word, one letter at a time. Not only was this a slow and painstaking process that disallowed the mass production of books in the modern sense, but it was also a process prone to errors. My students sometimes have difficulty believing that anybody copying a book by hand will necessarily make mistakes, and so I simply tell them, "Copy the Gospel of Matthew by hand and then compare it to a printed copy, and you'll see you make mistakes, even when you're trying not to. Even if you're a professional who does this for a living, mistakes will be made." This means, though, that in the ancient world, when there was more than one copy of a book, there was no guarantee that the multiple copies would be alike in all their details. Odds were that they would, in fact, be different from one another. It isn't like today when somebody writes a book, and the book gets reproduced in thousands of copies, and every copy is exactly alike. In the ancient world, when books were copied by hand, every version of the book, every copy of the book, would be slightly different, and some copies would be wildly different. When it comes to the Bible, this means when one of the books was being read in one location, it might be very different from the same book being read in a different location.

As it turns out, we don't have the original copies of any of the books of the New Testament—none of the letters of Paul, the Gospels, or the Apocalypse, in fact, of any early Christian text. The originals no longer survive. We're not sure why the early Christians didn't preserve the originals. Possibly, they didn't see that there would be a problem. Possibly, the originals themselves were used so frequently that they simply were worn out. Eventually, though, for one reason or another, they disappeared. They either were worn out, or thrown out, or they were destroyed. Since we don't have the originals of the New Testament, what do we have? We have copies. The vast majority of the copies were produced in centuries after the originals, from copies that were themselves also centuries removed from the originals, that had themselves been made from earlier copies. The copies that we have today range in date, from about the 2nd century beyond the invention of printing. So we have handwritten copies up through the 16th century.

With the invention of printing by movable type—the invention of the printing press by Guttenberg—you might expect that books would no longer be copied by hand, but in fact, it didn't work that way. Just as with the invention of the computer, people still sometimes use typewriters or, on those rare occasions, actually write something out by hand. The invention of the computer hasn't removed handwritten writing, for example, of letters in our age, just as the invention of the printing press didn't remove the production of manuscripts in its age. We have handwritten copies of books of the New Testament from after the invention of the printing press into the 16th century. They go back as far as the 2nd century, but not very far back into the 2nd century. Remember, the books of the New Testament themselves were produced, by and large, in the 1st century. The earliest copies we have of the books of the New Testament are copies that were on papyrus, which was an ancient writing material that was made out of the papyrus reed, which go along the banks of the Nile River. There was a manufacturing process, by which they could create a writing material out of papyrus; it was, in fact, a fairly sophisticated process, and papyrus made for a very good writing material. Our earliest manuscripts, the manuscripts from the 2nd and the 3rd centuries, up into the fourth century and somewhat beyond, in some instances, are written on papyrus.

Our very earliest manuscript of any book of the New Testament is, in fact, a little fragment that was discovered in a trash heap in Egypt. The fragment is the size of a credit card, and it has writing on both the front and the back of parts of verses from John, chapter 18. It's significant that this papyrus fragment has writing on the front and back because that shows that originally, this copy of the Gospel of John was written in a codex or in book form, rather than on a scroll. As you may know, in the ancient world, most literary texts were written on scrolls, but the early Christians, for some reason, preferred to write their documents, their books, in codex form, where you write on front and back of sheets and then stitch the sheets together into what is now the form of our books. This, our earliest fragment of the Gospel of John, was written in book form, codex form, rather than on a scroll.

It's difficult to date ancient papyri manuscripts, and the way that they're typically dated, actually, is by handwriting analysis. The fancy term for that is *paleography*, the study of ancient writing. On paleographical grounds, this particular papyrus can be dated to the first part of the 2nd century, so roughly maybe around the year 125 or the year 140. This papyrus is called P52, because it's the 52nd papyrus that has been cataloged by scholars who catalog such things. After the use of papyrus, starting in the 4th century, scribes copied their documents onto parchment manuscripts. Parchment is a writing material made out of animal skins, which was widely used until the widespread use of paper in early modern times. We have copies of the New Testament, but we don't have the originals. The earliest copy is simply of a few verses from the early 2nd century. We don't have complete books on any manuscript that survives until about the end of the 3rd century. We don't, in fact, have complete copies of the whole New Testament until the 4th century, 300 years after the books themselves were written.

We have thousands of copies that survived. Most of the copies that survived, however, are from the Middle Ages. New copies show up on occasion. At present, we have over 5,400 copies in Greek of the Greek New Testament, but the vast majority of these copies are from the Middle Ages, hundreds and hundreds of years after the originals. Sometimes you'll hear a Christian apologist argue that the New Testament can be trusted because we have more manuscripts of the New Testament than of any other book from the ancient world. Part of that is true; we do have more manuscripts of the New Testament than of any other book from the ancient world. That doesn't mean that the writings of the New Testament can be trusted; all that means is that we are better positioned to know what the words of the New Testament originally were than we are for most other books. That doesn't mean that the words are true. They may be true or they may not be true. We simply can't know what they are, in most instances; but in fact, in many instances it's difficult to know what the words are. The reason it's difficult to know what the words are—what the original words written by the authors are—is because of the differences found among these surviving copies.

How many differences are there among these copies? It's a striking phenomenon that among these 5,400 or so copies of the New Testament that we have, no two are exactly alike in all their wording. There are differences among all of these surviving copies, which means, probably, that all of them embody mistakes. One task of scholars is to try to reconstruct what the original author said, given the fact that we don't have the originals, and we don't have copies that embody the text of the originals. Scribes that copied the Christians texts, including those of the New Testament, obviously changed their texts. This leads to a host of interesting questions that we'll be addressing in this lecture. Why were the originals of the New Testament changed in copying? How extensive are the changes? If all of the copies have mistakes, are there places where we don't know what the authors originally wrote?

The fact that the originals don't survive and that we have mistakes in copies was occasionally noted in the Middle Ages. But it wasn't until relatively modern times that this was recognized as a major problem that had to be dealt with. Occasionally, you'll have some Christian author, even in the ancient world, who would say, "Well, different manuscripts have different wordings for this verse." Nobody really recognized the extent of the problem until modern times. Sometimes, scribes themselves recognized the problem.

There's a famous manuscript called *Codex Vaticanus*; it's called that because it was found in the Vatican library. It's a very extensive manuscript of the New Testament that's a high-quality manuscript from the 4th century. There's this interesting phenomenon in *Codex Vaticanus*. In the book of Hebrews, there's a passage, Hebrews, chapter 1, verse 3, which says, "Christ manifests all things by the word of his power." That's actually what the scribe of *Codex Vaticanus* wrote. The problem is that other manuscripts at that place read something slightly different. They say, "Christ bears all things by the word of his power." It's a word that looks similar in Greek; the word is *pherone* instead of the word *phonerone*. A scribe came along after *Vaticanus* was done, and was reading through *Codex Vaticanus,* and saw that he wrote a different word in this place. The scribe erased the word *manifests* and put in the words *bears*, a similar-sounding word.

A few centuries later another scribe came along, and saw what the previous scribal corrector had done; he erased the word *bears,* and wrote back the word *manifests,* and then wrote a marginal note between the columns. His marginal note says, "Fool and knave, leave the old reading, don't change it." I think this is a wonderful illustration of how scribes were changing the manuscripts, and how some scribes got perturbed by it. I actually have a copy of this page framed, sitting above my desk in my study, because I think it's such a wonderful illustration of scribal changes of the text.

Scholars didn't recognize how extensively the manuscripts of the New Testament were different from one another until the early 18th century. The major breakthrough came in the year 1707 with the publication of an edition of the Greek New Testament by an Oxford scholar named John Mill—who is, I think, unrelated to the later Victorian scholar, John Stuart Mill. John

Mill, in the early 18th century, had actually spent 30 years of his life comparing the Greek manuscripts that were available to him. He also looked at the ancient translation of the New Testament into other languages—Latin, Syriac, Coptic—ancient versions of the New Testament, to see what their text said at different places; and he looked at how the New Testament was quoted by church fathers, to see what their manuscripts must have looked like in their own day. Mill compiled the results of these collates of these manuscripts, and he published an edition of the New Testament in 1707 that included an apparatus of variant readings that he discovered. In other words, he printed the text and underneath the text, he indicated places where he had found differences among the manuscripts. He only included the differences that he found to be significant; he didn't include everything that he found.

To the shock and dismay of Mill's contemporaries, Mill's apparatus indicated 30,000 places of variation among the manuscript. There were 30,000 places where the manuscripts that he had examined differed from one another in their wording of the text. Remember, these are only the places that he thought were significant. A number of Mill's readers were upset by the publication of this apparatus, and some of the more pious claimed that Mill was working to render the text of scripture uncertain. Mill's defenders pointed out that Mill hadn't invented these places of variation; he had simply noticed that they existed, so he really couldn't be blamed for doing anything wrong. But 30,000 places of variation—that sounds fairly significant, and yet scholars since the early 18th century have discovered many, many, more variant readings among our surviving manuscripts, as manuscripts continued to be discovered, even down until today. Today people are still discovering manuscripts. Mill had examined about 100 manuscripts of the New Testament; today we have well over 5,000. We have 50 times more manuscripts than he had.

How many variant readings do we know about? How many places of variation survive to our knowledge? The reality is no one knows how many variant readings there are among the manuscripts of the New Testament, because nobody has been able to count them all. Even with computers, at this point, we still don't know. Some people put the number at 200,000; some say 300,000. I'm not sure how many there are, but perhaps it's easiest to put the number in comparative terms. There are more variants in our manuscripts than there are words in the New Testament—that's a lot of variations. Now, I should say that most of these variations are completely insignificant, and of no bearing on anything. The majority of these simply show that scribes in antiquity could spell no better than most people can today and, of course, this was in the world before there was spell check. There weren't even dictionaries, so of course scribes can't really be blamed for that. But a lot of the differences are simply blunders in spelling, and every blunder in spelling is a variant reading.

There are lots of other accidental changes that one finds in manuscripts, where scribes simply messed up. They were tired, they were inept, they were inattentive, or for whatever reason, they simply made mistakes—not just spelling differences, but differences such as the change of word order, where they leave out a word and stick it in later. Sometimes they'll accidentally leave out a word; sometimes a scribe will accidentally leave out a line. If you have two lines of a text that end with the same words, for example, in Jesus' parable, he'll say something about the angels of Heaven. And then a little bit later, he'll say the angels of Heaven. If both angels of Heaven occur at the end of a line, then a scribe sometimes would copy the first angels of Heaven; but then when his eye went back to the page, it would alight on the second occurrence of the angels in Heaven, and he would start copying from there; and thereby, he would leave out the intervening line. When lines end the same way, the technical term for that is *homoeoteleuton*, meaning they end in the same way. When the scribe has an eye skip, where his eye skips to the wrong place, it's called *parablepsis*. This kind of mistake is called parablepsis occasioned by homoeoteleuton, as I try to teach my students to recite. There are lots of accidental changes.

Sometimes scribes would leave out an entire page. Probably the most bizarre set of accidental changes in a manuscript in is a 14th-century manuscript that is called Manuscript 109. The scribe of Manuscript 109 really blew it at one point in his manuscript, specifically in the place in Luke's Gospel where Luke is giving the genealogy of Jesus. If you remember in Luke's genealogy, Luke traces Jesus' line back through Joseph—so–and-so begat so–and-so, and begat so-and-so—traces it all the way back to Adam, who is then said to be the Son of God. The scribe of Manuscript 109, apparently, was copying a manuscript in which the genealogy was given in two columns, so it had one column on the left, and then the second column on the right continuing the genealogy; but the column on the right didn't go to the bottom of the page. This scribe, not paying attention to what he was doing, instead of copying the first column and then the second column, copied across the columns. He copied the first line of the first column, and then the first line of the second column, the second line of the first column, and then the second line of the second column, and so forth down the line, which led to some very interesting results. Since the second column didn't go to the bottom of the page, the second column ends by saying the son of Adam is the Son of God. In this manuscript, it turns out that God is the son of Eram, and the father of the entire human race isn't Adam; it's a man named Farise. This scribe wasn't paying attention. There are lots of accidental mistakes in our manuscripts. In most instances, like this particular one of Manuscript 109, it's fairly simple to detect what the problem is.

Sometimes, though, it's difficult to know what the problem is. This is especially the case in places where it looks like a scribe did not accidentally make a mistake, but where a scribe intentionally changed the text. There are passages that look like scribes have intentionally modified the texts that they were copying. Let me give you some of the more important textual variations that are quite significant for interpreting the New Testament, where it really matters what the original text was because you have different forms of the text, and depending on which form of the text you have, the text reads very differently.

Possibly the most famous is the well-known story of John, chapter 8, of Jesus and the adulteress. This could well be the best-known event in the life of Jesus; it certainly makes it into every Jesus movie ever made. Even Mel Gibson's *Passion*, which is about Jesus' last hours, includes it in one of the flashbacks. It is about the potential stoning of the adulteress. You know the story: Jesus is teaching in the temple, and the scribes and Pharisees bring a woman to him. They say to him, this woman was caught in the act of adultery. According to the Law of Moses, she is to be stoned to death. What do you say? Jesus kneels down in the ground and starts writing in the dirt, and then they keep questioning him. He looks up and he says, "Let the one without sin among you be the first to cast a stone at her." Then he continues writing, and they eventually start leaving, apparently because they realize their own guilt. They leave one by one, and when Jesus looks up, there's nobody there except for the woman. He looks up and says to the woman, "Is there no one left to condemn you?" She says, "No, Lord, no one." He says, "Neither do I condemn you. Go and sin no more." It's a very interesting story. It shows Jesus' kind of cleverness at getting out of a trap because he can't very well say, "Don't stone her," because then he'd be saying, "Don't follow the Law of Moses," which he can't say. On the other hand, he can't say, "Stone her," because that violates his teachings of mercy and forgiveness. So he's kind of stuck in this situation; they've trapped him, but he figures a way out of a trap. It's a very clever story.

There are odd features of this story. For one thing, if this woman is caught in the act of adultery, where's the man? The Law says you're supposed to stone both of them to death. It's got some odd characteristics in it. What's most odd, though, is that the story was not originally found in the Gospel of John; it now occurs in John, chapter 8. In fact, in the oldest manuscripts of the Gospel of John, the story does not occur at all. Moreover, in some manuscripts, the story occurs in the Gospel of Luke. In a number of manuscripts the story occurs, but it occurs with a kind of an asterisk, indicating that the scribe doesn't think that it's original. When you read the story in Greek, the writing style is completely different from the writing style of the rest of the Gospel of John. When you take the story out of the Gospel of John, and you read from where it begins to where it ends, the flow of John makes perfect sense, much better sense than it does with the story in it. What's going on here? Apparently, some scribe knew of this story, had heard this story, and decided to write it out in the margin of a manuscript. Some later scribe saw this marginal note and thought it belonged in the text, and so stuck it in the text. Later scribes, then, copied that manuscript. The oldest manuscripts don't have the story, but the manuscripts used by the King James Bible translators, those manuscripts did have the story. That's why it came into the English language—because the King James translators were using late manuscripts that were not our best manuscripts. They reproduced the story even though it was not originally found in the Gospel of John. This is not actually a story that was found in the original canon of the New Testament.

A second example: the Gospel of Mark has a very interesting ending. Jesus has been crucified and buried. On the third day, the women go to the tomb, but they find the tomb empty. They see a man there in the tomb, and the man tells them to go tell the disciples that Jesus will go before them to Galilee; they're to meet him there. Jesus has been raised; they're to meet him in Galilee. Mark, chapter 16, verse 8 says, "But the women fled the tomb and didn't say anything to anyone, for they were afraid." That's where the Gospel ends in the oldest and best manuscripts. The women don't tell anybody, and Jesus never appears to the disciples—boom, end of story. This is a fascinating ending; it's a brilliant ending for the Gospel of Mark, where nobody can figure out who Jesus is, and at the end, they still don't figure out who he is, because they're not told that he's been raised from the dead—terrific ending. Some scribes, though, were really taken up short when they got to that ending and thought—wait a second, Jesus surely appeared to people, surely there were resurrection appearances. And so, a number of scribes added endings to the Gospel of Mark, including the ending that's found in most of our English Bibles. With the story of the woman taken in adultery, in most modern English Bibles, you'll find that this ending is put in brackets. The translator's telling you this is not an original ending, but is an ending that's been added on.

In the added-on ending, there are 12 verses in which Jesus appears to his disciples. In these verses, he tells them to go make disciples of all the nations, and he says that anybody who believes in his name will drink deadly poison, and they'll take up deadly snakes, and they won't hurt them. This is the passage that Appalachian snake handlers use to justify their handling of poisonous snakes. The problem is that it wasn't originally in the Gospel of Mark; this is a later scribal addition. No wonder some of these people end up in the hospital; it's not part of the Bible, this is a later addition. The Gospel of Mark originally ended with the women fleeing the tomb because they were afraid.

In the Gospel of Luke, we saw that, when Jesus is being nailed to the cross, he prays to God, "Father, forgive them, for they don't know what they're doing." There's an interesting variant at this point. In some of our best manuscripts, Jesus doesn't pray this prayer. Why would a scribe change the text? Why would a scribe add that prayer? It's interesting that in the early church this prayer was interpreted for God to forgive the Jews for their guilt in turning Jesus over to be executed. If that's how it's interpreted, it's not surprising that scribes took it out. Scribes, in an age that had grown increasingly anti-Jewish, didn't want Jesus to pray for the forgiveness of the Jews, since God obviously hadn't forgiven the Jews, so they took out Jesus' prayer for the Jews.

A final example in Mark, chapter 1, Jesus is approached by a leper in order to be healed. It says that Jesus felt compassion for him and healed him. But in some manuscripts, it says that Jesus got angry and healed him. Jesus got angry? Many scholars think that's the original text, and their logic is, if a scribe is copying that text, are they more likely to change the text from saying Jesus felt compassion for the man to make him say he got angry, or are they more likely to take a text that said he got angry, and change it to say Jesus felt compassion? The latter is more likely; therefore, that's likely the way the scribal change went, which means, originally, the text probably said that Jesus felt anger and then healed the man, and scribes changed it to say that Jesus felt compassion.

How do scholars make the decisions, though, about which text is original? Scholars use a number of criteria. They look at which manuscripts are the oldest manuscripts that survived. They look to see which readings are found in a wide range of manuscripts, found in a number of geographical locations. They look at which reading conforms most closely to the vocabulary and theology of the author. They see which reading is likely that a scribe created—is it likely the scribe made Jesus angry or that the scribe made Jesus compassionate? The reading that's more difficult is the one that the scribe probably did not invent. The more difficult reading is probably the original reading, in most cases.

Using these and other criteria, scholars are confident that in most cases, we can be reasonably sure what the authors of the New Testament originally wrote, but there will always be places where we're not sure. It's important to remember that when we read the New Testament, we're not reading the originals produced by the ancient authors; we're reading translations into English of Greek texts whose originals didn't survive. These translations are based on copies of the originals, and all of these copies have errors in them. In some places, we may not even know what an author originally said.

Lecture Ten
Authority in the Early Church

Scope: The need to have written authorities for faith and practice is ultimately what drove Christians to construct a *canon* of Scripture—that is, a collection of books that were seen to be authoritative for what to believe and how to live. From the very beginning, Christians already had one canon in that they accepted the books of the Jewish Scriptures (the Christian Old Testament) as an authoritative account of God's word. But soon there was a need for additional, distinctively Christian authorities, and this is what led Christians to consider some of the writings of the apostles (such as Paul and the authors of the Gospels) as standing on an equal footing with the writings of the Old Testament.

But given the varying understandings of the Christian religion, there were a variety of books from which to choose. How did Christian leaders know which books to include in this "New" Testament?

Outline

I. In the last lecture, we noted that the early Christian writings were in wide circulation, but we haven't explored yet the more basic question of why they were so widely circulated.

    A. This may seem like an obvious question, but it is one that rarely gets asked.

        1. Why were the Christians so interested in the literature being produced in the early years of the religion?

        2. Why did some of this literature come to take on a kind of sacred status among Christians?

        3. And when did this happen?

    B. One reason this question does not get asked much is that people today simply assume that religions are rooted in religious texts; thus, Christianity would have been as well, from the beginning.

    C. But the idea that a religion would be rooted in sacred texts was virtually unheard of in the Roman world.

        1. Roman religions were not textually based.

2. In Christian circles, Christianity is thought about in doctrinal terms (beliefs).

3. Roman religions were not rooted in belief, but in practice: It was the worship of the gods that mattered, not what one believed about the gods.

4. These religions were rooted around the idea that what mattered in life were the things that the gods controlled, and humans could not, such as rain, and good health.

5. Roman religions were based on present life, not on afterlife. Most people in the ancient world did not believe in an afterlife; for them, the purpose of religion was to guarantee quality of life in the present.

6. Religions in the ancient world were polytheistic, and designed to maintain peace with the gods.

7. The one partial exception, of course, was Judaism. Judaism was monotheistic, practice-based, more than belief-based, and had a sacred Scripture.

8. And the Jews' sacred Scripture soon became the Christians' sacred Scripture.

9. But why did Christians begin to regard other writings also as Scripture?

10. We will consider the entire process by which a group of Christian books became the sacred canon of the New Testament in our final lecture. In this lecture, we will consider the broader question of why Christians sought written authorities in the first place.

II. The place to begin is with one of the truly exceptional features of Christianity in the Roman world. This was an exclusivistic religion.

   A. Exclusivistic religions were virtually unknown in the polytheistic world of the Roman Empire.

   B. Even Judaism is only a partial exception, because not even Jews were eager to convert others to their own faith.

   C. But from the beginning, Christians insisted that there was only one right religion, only one way to be right with the one true God, and only one set of beliefs that could be acceptable to him.

   D. The belief in Jesus as the messiah became the *sine qua non* for Christians at the earliest stages of the religion.

E.   This means that belief and its corollary, knowledge, became central to the early Christian Church.

F.   Anyone with the wrong beliefs or the wrong knowledge was, therefore, estranged from God.

G.   As a result, it was imperative to have the right beliefs and the right knowledge.

III. Christianity became a text-based religion because it was a belief-based religion.

A.   If what mattered was proper beliefs, one needed to know what things to believe.

B.   This, in turn, presupposed having authority for knowing what to believe.

C.   The ultimate authority, of course, was Jesus. After his death, authority naturally descended upon his disciples. But as they were scattered and eventually died, what could take their place as authorities? The answer was: The books they left behind.

IV. Problems arose as different Christian groups believing different things all claimed to have the correct understanding of the religion (that is, claimed to represent the views of Jesus and his followers).

A.   One of the most important "discoveries" of modern scholarship is that early Christianity was, in fact, remarkably diverse in its beliefs.

B.   The various beliefs of Christians into the 2nd and 3rd centuries make the modern-day diversity of Christian denominations and theologies pale by comparison.

C.   We can see this variety of early beliefs by exploring the ideas of two significant Christian groups of the 2nd century.

   1.   The Ebionites maintained that Jesus was the Jewish messiah sent from the Jewish God to the Jewish people; as a righteous man (and only a man), he had been chosen by God to die for the sake of others, but he was not himself divine or born of a virgin.

   2.   The Marcionites maintained that the Jewish God was not the God of Jesus but was a God of wrath who had created this miserable world, then condemned people for not keeping his Law. Jesus came from a different, good God to save people

from the Jewish God of wrath. He was not actually human (belonging to this creation) but was himself completely divine.

    3. Why didn't the Ebionites and the Marcionites simply read the New Testament to see that their views were wrong? Because the New Testament did not exist yet. It came into existence as a response to these conflicts, not prior to them.

D. It is striking that each of these groups actually claimed scriptural authority for their views.

    1. The Ebionites had something like Matthew, the most "Jewish" of our Gospels, and rejected Paul as an arch-heretic.

    2. The Marcionites had something like our Luke, the most "non-Jewish" of our Gospels, and accepted Paul as the ultimate authority.

E. Eventually, both groups were declared heretical, and a different view emerged as victorious that agreed on some points with both groups and disagreed vehemently on others. It was this group that gave us the Scriptures that are accepted as canonical today (as we'll see in Lecture Twelve).

V. In sum, Christianity became a text-based religion because it invoked the need for proper belief, and proper belief required proper knowledge, and proper knowledge required established authorities, and authorities that are written are, in theory, more "certain" than those that are merely spoken, because their words are then cast in permanent form, available to anyone with eyes to see.

Essential Reading:

Bart D. Ehrman, *The New Testament: A Historical Introduction to the Early Christian Writings*, chapter 1.

————, *The Orthodox Corruption of Scripture: The Effect of Early Christological Controversies on the Text of the New Testament*, chapter 1.

Supplementary Reading:

Walter Bauer, *Orthodoxy and Heresy in Earliest Christianity*.

Bart D. Ehrman, *Lost Christianities: The Battles for Scripture and Faiths We Never Knew*.

Harry Gamble, *The New Testament Canon: Its Making and Meaning*.

Questions to Consider:

1. Why do you suppose today that people simply assume that all major religions are based on sacred texts?

2. If Christianity from early times was "text-based," why do you suppose Christians didn't go to greater lengths to copy the surviving texts accurately?

Lecture Ten—Transcript
Authority in the Early Church

In the last lecture, we noted that the early Christian writings were in wide circulation. But we haven't explored yet the more basic question of why they were so widely circulated. This may seem like an obvious question, but it's one that rarely gets asked. Why were the Christians so interested in the literature being produced in the early years of the religion? Why did some of this literature come to take on a kind of sacred status among Christians? When did this happen?

One reason this question does not get asked much is that people today simply assume that religions are rooted in religious texts; thus Christianity would have been as well, from the beginning. The idea that a religion would be rooted in sacred texts was virtually unheard of in the Roman world. To make sense of this, we have to know something about Roman religions, which in fact were not, as a rule, textually based religions. Roman religion was very different from the kind of religion people are accustomed to thinking about today, especially in Christian circles. In Christian circles, religion is often thought about in doctrinal terms. Being a Christian is dependent upon what one believes. One must believe in one God; one must believe in Jesus his son; one must believe that Jesus died for the sins of the world, and was raised from the dead. Christianity, in many of its manifestations, is a religion rooted in belief. Roman religions—as odd as this may seem to modern people—Roman religions were not rooted in belief. Roman religions were rooted in practice. It was the worship of the Gods that mattered, not what one believed about the Gods. This is hard for many people to understand; my students simply have trouble getting their minds around it. The fact is, for most Roman religions it didn't matter what you believed. It simply mattered how you practiced the religion.

Now, of course to some extent, religious practices are based on belief. But what was really central to the Roman religions were the sacrifices performed to the Gods and the prayers said to the Gods—often set prayers said to the Gods. The religions were rooted around the idea that what mattered in life were things that the Gods could provide. The humans themselves were unable to provide for themselves. Humans, in fact, are limited in what they can provide for themselves. We can't guarantee rain for the crops; we can't guarantee health; we can't guarantee that our village or our town will be victorious over the next village or town; we can't guarantee that women will survive childbirth, or that children will survive childbirth; we can't guarantee that there'll be food available for us or water. There are things that are beyond our control. In the ancient world, religions were rooted around the idea that the gods could provide things that were beyond human control. The gods were worshipped so that the gods would provide what is needed.

These religions were almost completely based on present life, rather than afterlife. Many Christians today are more concerned about afterlife than present life in terms of their religion. They want to believe the right things, so they go to Heaven rather than go to Hell. This was not a concern for most people in the ancient world. Most people in the ancient world simply didn't believe in an afterlife; most people believed that when you died, that was end of the story. So the concern of the religion wasn't to guarantee an afterlife; it was to guarantee life in the present—a life that was very tenuous on its own terms. The Gods, however, could provide what was needed.

All of the Roman religions were entirely polytheistic. The only exception—that we'll see in a second—was Judaism. All of the other religions were polytheistic, worshipping many gods. For Romans, and for Greeks before them, and for everybody else in the ancient world, the idea that there were many gods was simply commonsensical. Today people might think that the choice is between whether you believe in God or don't believe in God, so that the choice is monotheism or no theism. In the ancient world, it didn't work that way. In the ancient world, everybody knew that there were many gods; there were gods of all sorts of functions and of all sorts of places. There were gods of locations, gods of the forest, gods of the streams, gods of the villages, gods of the home, gods of the hearth. There were gods of all occasions and of all functions. There were gods who made the crops grow, gods who gave wealth, gods who gave health, and gods who provided people with what they needed for their daily lives, including health, and prosperity, and love, and every other function. There were gods who looked over childbirth, gods who looked over the livestock, and gods for every purpose you could imagine. For the ancient people, the idea that there could only be one God was silly, and ridiculous, and to be mocked. And so anybody who was a monotheist—in other words, the Jews—were mocked for thinking there's only one God. That seemed ridiculous to ancient people. Saying you can have only one god is like saying you can have only one friend or one acquaintance. There are a lots of people in the world and, of course, you can know as many as you want—same with the gods.

In these polytheistic Roman religions, the gods were worshipped by sacrifice of animals and through prayers, to guarantee that the gods would provide what was needed in the present life, not in order to guarantee an afterlife. The religious practice—the *cultus deorum* as it's called, the "care of the gods," or the religious cult—was designed in order to guarantee the peace among the gods, peace between people and the gods, so the gods would provide what's needed. It was not understood that these gods were jealous. Gods were not jealous of one another, except in the mythology that most people accepted simply as being good stories, not being as sacred scripture or religious text, per se. People understood that the gods were at peace with one another, and harmony with one another, and various gods could be worshipped, and other gods wouldn't be jealous about it. The emphasis was on practice rather than belief. It was on present life, rather than afterlife. The emphasis was on the peace of the gods and on the need to make sacrifices and prayers, so that the gods would provide what was needed.

These religions were not textually based; Roman religions didn't have a Bible comparable to what Christianity later had, and Judaism, to some extent, had. The one exception, then, is Judaism among the Roman religions. Judaism was different from the other religions in that it was monotheistic. It maintained that there was only one God who is to be worshipped by his devotees, so that if you followed the God of Israel, you couldn't worship other gods. It was also practice-based more than belief-based. It was a religion of religious practices, practices such as the rite of circumcision. They had certain food laws that had to be followed (keeping kosher); certain festival days that were to be observed to God; sacrifices that were to be made to God; one day of the week in which one is to rest and reflect upon God. Judaism, unlike the other religions, also had a sacred scripture. This was a set of books that indicated God's will for his people, that gave the laws concerning sacrifices and other aspects of worship, and laws that dictated how people were to relate to one another as the people of God.

Judaism, then, had a set of sacred texts, which became the Hebrew Bible, what Christians today call the Old Testament. This means that when Christianity appeared on the scene, since Christianity started out as a sect within Judaism, it inherited a set of scriptures. The earliest Christians did have scriptures, namely, the Jewish scriptures that eventually became the Old Testament as soon as Christians developed a separate set of scriptures that they called the New Testament. Why did Christians begin to regard other writings besides the Hebrew Bible as scripture? That's the question we'll be dealing with in this lecture and the final lecture of this course. We will consider the entire process by which a group of distinctively Christian books became the sacred canon of scripture. That will be the last lecture of the course.

In this particular lecture, I want to consider the broader question of why Christians sought written authorities for their religion in the first place. The place to begin is with one of the truly exceptional features of Christianity in the Roman world. Christianity, unlike the other Roman religions, was an exclusivistic religion. In other words, Christianity insisted that it was right and since it was the right religion, all other religions were wrong. This point of view, this exclusivistic perspective, was virtually unknown among the polytheistic religions of the ancient world.

As I indicated, in Roman religions, it was almost everywhere recognized that the gods were not jealous of one another, so that if you worshipped Zeus, it didn't mean that you couldn't also worship Athena; and if you worshipped Athena, you couldn't worship your local city gods; if you worshipped your local city gods, that didn't mean you couldn't worship your family gods; if you worshipped your family gods, that didn't mean that you couldn't accept some other new deity, to worship that deity as well. You could worship as many gods as you wanted. Roman religions were not exclusivistic. They did not insist that if they were right, other religions were wrong. Even Judaism is only a partial exception to this rule because Jews did subscribe to their own religion, and they thought that their religion was right for Jews; but Jews, by and large, were not concerned to convert other people to believe in Judaism. Jews expected that other people would worship their gods in a way that was appropriate to their gods, and they, the Jews, would worship their God in the way that was appropriate to them. But Jews, by and large, did not constitute a missionary religion. Judaism was not missionary in the sense that it tried to convert other people to believe in its faith, because that wasn't its ultimate concern.

Christianity, though, was different. From the very beginning, Christians insisted that their religion was the only right religion. Christians maintained that Jesus was the Jewish Messiah, sent from the Jewish God to the Jewish people in fulfillment of the Jewish scriptures; and the only way to be right with this Jewish God, who is the only true God, is by accepting Jesus. Someone who did not have faith in Jesus could not be right with the God who created this world, which meant they were worshipping a false religion. Christians insisted, then, that there's only one way to be right with God. There's only one God, there's only one way to be right with him, and that's belief in Jesus. So that belief in Jesus as the Messiah constituted the only right religion, the only way to be right with God. There is only one set of beliefs that could be acceptable to this God. Christianity started out as a religion of belief more than a religion of practice.

Now, I don't mean to say that Christians didn't have Christian practices. There were all sorts of Christian practices involved in the religion, practices of baptism and of Eucharist. They had worship services; they had sermons; they had scriptures readings; they had things that they did—there were Christian practices. But the religion, at its heart, emphasized belief far more than any other religion in the Roman Empire, even more than Judaism. For Christianity, beliefs were primary. So the belief in Jesus as the Messiah became the *sine qua non* at the earliest stages of their religion. This means that belief and its corollary knowledge were central to the early Christian Church in ways that simply didn't exist in Roman pagan religions. For Christians, anyone with the wrong beliefs or the wrong knowledge was, therefore, estranged from God. Because it's a belief-based religion that is exclusivistic—there's only one way to be right with God, namely, to have the right beliefs—it emphasized that the wrong beliefs and the wrong knowledge lead to estrangement from God. As a result, it was imperative to have the right beliefs, the right knowledge.

With Christianity, there came onto the religious scene the possibility of orthodoxy and heresy. *Orthodoxy* is a word that literally means "correct belief." *Heresy* comes from a Greek word that means "choice." A *heretic* is somebody who chooses not to believe the right beliefs. Of course, as you might understand, these terms are a little bit complicated historically because in actual fact, nobody thinks that they believe the wrong beliefs. If somebody believes they believe the wrong beliefs, they would believe something else; they would accept the right beliefs. Nobody thinks they're wrong because if they thought they were wrong, they would change their views. So nobody actually thinks that they are a heretic. Everybody thinks that they are orthodox, by definition. Within Christianity, though, there developed a sense that there is one right belief, that's orthodoxy, and alternative forms of belief were heresy. Heresy was to be rejected because heresy can lead to damnation. If what matters to the religion is proper belief, as with the case in early Christianity, then one needed to know what things to believe.

This idea that there could be orthodoxy and a right belief, in turn, presupposed the need to have an authority for knowing what to believe. The ultimate authority, of course, was Jesus himself. After his death, authority naturally descended upon Jesus' disciples, who had known Jesus and could communicate his teachings. But as Jesus' disciples were scattered and eventually they died, what could take the place as authorities for the right Christian belief? The answer that Christians came up with was that their authorities were the books that the apostles left behind. Apostolic books became central to Christianity because authority mattered in a religion that stressed the importance of orthodoxy.

Problems arose, however, in early Christianity, as different Christian groups, believing different things, all claimed to have the correct understanding of the religion. That is, different groups all claimed to be orthodox, and what is striking is, all of these groups that have different beliefs could claim apostolic support for their beliefs. They could claim that their beliefs, in fact, were authorized by written texts that they had. That created a problem. It's this problem that you have different Christian groups with different beliefs with different books, all claiming to authorize those different beliefs, all competing with one another. It's that problem that eventually leads to the formation of a Christian canon of scripture—a collection of books that all Christians can agree on, that these are our sacred texts that authorize correct belief. As we're going to see in the next lecture, even having the correct books didn't solve the problem of diversity among early Christians because having a book isn't the same as interpreting a book. And different people can interpret the same book in different ways; but at least if you have the same books in common, you can have a common ground for arguing out what correct belief is. So it became important for Christians to agree on which books were going to be sacred scripture within the religion.

One of the most important discoveries of modern scholarship, in fact, wasn't a discovery in the sands of Egypt of some ancient text, it was a discovery actually made in the libraries of Europe. It's a discovery that early Christianity was, in fact, remarkably diverse in its beliefs. The various beliefs of Christians into the 2nd and 3rd centuries make the modern diversity of Christian denominations and theologies pale by comparison. There were Christians who believed a wide range of things, all of them claiming that they represented the views of Jesus. In the 2nd and 3rd centuries, there were Christians who said, of course, that there is only one God. There were Christians in the 2nd and 3rd centuries, though, that said that there were two gods. Some Christians in the 2nd and 3rd centuries said there were 30 gods. We know one Christian group that maintained there were 365 gods. Christians? How could they be Christian if they believed in 365 gods? Because they said, that's what Jesus taught. Well, how would they think that? Because they had books that said that's what Jesus taught. Christians? Well, at the time they called themselves Christians. We know of Christians in the 2nd and 3rd centuries who believed that God created the world. There are other Christians who said that God didn't create this world; an evil deity created this world. There were Christians in the 2nd and 3rd centuries who said Jesus was both human and divine. Some Christians, though, said Jesus was human, but he was not divine. Others said that he's divine, but he's not human. How could they be Christian? Because they said that's what Jesus himself taught and they had books that could prove it. There were some Christians who said that Jesus' death brought about the salvation of the world. Other Christians said that Jesus' death had nothing to do with the salvation of the world. For example, there's the Gospel of Thomas, where the death of Jesus doesn't matter for salvation. There were other Christians that said that Jesus never actually died. Christians had a wide range of belief in early Christianity, and the debates among Christians is what eventually led to the formation of an authorized set of books that could establish once and for all, in theory, what Christians were to believe.

I want to explore a little bit further the variety of early Christian beliefs by looking at two significant Christian groups of the 2nd century—just to illustrate my point of how diverse early Christianity was, and how authorities became central for the understanding of early Christianity, and for their understanding of Christian belief. The first group I want to talk about is a group called the Ebionites. This was a group of 2nd-century Christians who claimed to represent the original Christian view.

The Ebionites acquired their name from the enemies, apparently, who called them Ebionites. They may have called themselves Ebionites, but it's a little bit hard to know because we don't have any writings that are directly from Ebionites. Most scholars think that the word *Ebionite* actually comes from the Hebrew word, *'ebyon*, which means "poor." They may have called themselves "the poor ones" because they may have imitated Jesus' followers in voluntarily giving up their possessions for the sake of others. Their enemies called them "the poor ones" because their enemies said that they were poor in faith. In other words, they had the wrong beliefs.

These Ebionites were a group of Jewish Christians who maintained the Jewish focus of the Christian religion. Ebionites were personally Jewish—the men were circumcised, the men and the women kept the Jewish Law, they kept kosher, they kept Sabbath, and they kept some Jewish festivals. They were strict monotheists who believed that Jesus was the Jewish Messiah who was sent from the Jewish God to the Jewish people in fulfillment of the Jewish Law, and that the religion, therefore, was Jewish. Anybody who wanted to be a follower of the religion also had to be Jewish; anyone who was a follower of Jesus had, like Jesus, to keep the Jewish Law.

Who was Jesus for these people? According to the Ebionites, Jesus was the most righteous man who had ever lived; Jesus was one who actually kept the Law of God perfectly. He was a Jew; he was born a Jew, and in fact, he was born by natural means. Jesus was not born of a virgin. He did not exist before his birth. Jesus was born through the sexual union of Joseph and Mary. He was born like everybody else is born, but he was more righteous than anyone else; and because he was more righteous than any one else, God chose him to be his Messiah, the one who would die for the sake of others. God gave Jesus a commission to die for the sins of others and Jesus fulfilled his commission by dying on the cross. God accepted the sacrifice for sins and forgave other people because of Jesus' perfect sacrifice. Jesus, in other words, was a human being. He was not divine, he was not God; he was thoroughly a man, a righteous Jewish man, the most righteous man ever to have lived. Salvation comes by believing in his death.

These Ebionites, then, represented a sect within Christianity. I call them a sect because they were a separate group within Christianity, because most Christians rejected the Ebionites' claims. They didn't reject all the claims. Most Christians agreed that Jesus was a righteous man who kept the Law. But Christians eventually came to think that Jesus was born of a virgin. He wasn't just a man, he was also divine. Where did the Ebionites get their ideas, though, that Jesus was just a man, that he wasn't divine, and that people should keep the Jewish Law? Why didn't they simply read the New Testament to see that these views were wrong? The answer, of course, is that the New Testament didn't exist yet.

The Ebionites had sacred books; one that we know about was a Gospel. One of the Gospels that the Ebionites used was a Gospel that was very much like our Gospel of Matthew. If you recall, Matthew is the most Jewish of our Gospels. In Matthew's Gospel, the emphasis is on Jesus' Jewish-ness, his descent from Abraham, his fulfillment of the Jewish Law, and his insistence that others keep the Jewish Law. This was a book that was used by the Ebionites, although they appear to have modified the Gospel of Matthew because they eliminated chapters 1 and 2, which are the two chapters that describe Jesus' virgin birth. Their Gospel of Matthew didn't have that narrative in it. Those are the Ebionites, one sect within early Christianity.

The second group I want to describe stood over against the Ebionites; it's a group that is called the Marcionites. The Marcionites are called Marcionites for a distinct reason; they were followers of a 2nd-century philosopher teacher named Marcion. Marcion was a Christian thinker who maintained that the apostle Paul was the one who really had it right. The apostle Paul, as we have seen in our discussion of the Letter to the Galatians, indicated that a person is made right with God not by keeping the Jewish Law, but by having faith in Christ. Marcion pushed this distinction between the Law, on the one hand, and the Gospel of Christ, on the other hand, to what we saw as a logical extreme. The God of the Jews described in the Jewish Bible, the God who gave the Law, is not the God who gives the Gospel. There is a difference between the God of the Old Testament, the God of wrath, and the God of love and mercy proclaimed by Jesus. If God is a God of wrath and justice, as described in the Old Testament, in the Hebrew Bible, he can't very well also be the God of love, and mercy, and forgiveness that Jesus described. Why is that? It is because they are two separate Gods. Jesus does not come from the God who chose Israel to be his people, who created this world in the first place; Jesus comes from a different God. Jesus came to save people from the harsh, wrathful God of the Old Testament. Marcion, in other words, was not a monotheist, he was a ditheist; he believed in two separate gods. The one true God was unknown to this world until Jesus appeared. This version of Christianity is completely anti-Jewish: it rejects the God of the Jews, and it rejects his Law, and it insists that Christians not follow the Law, claiming Paul as the ultimate authority. Now, as you might imagine, Paul was, in fact, the enemy of the Ebionites in their view. The Ebionites, who were Jewish Christians, saw Paul as the archenemy because he taught that salvation comes apart from the Law. The Ebionites thought that salvation came by keeping the Law. Not the Marcionites, though. The Marcionites saw Paul as the real hero of the faith. They were ditheists who were anti-Jewish.

According to the Marcionites, who was Jesus? Jesus could not actually belong to the creator God, according the Marcionites, because he came from the other God. How is it, then, that he came into the world? According to the Marcionites, Jesus could not have been born of the sexual union of Joseph and Mary because that would make him a creature like other creatures; it would make him belong to the material world. Christ, then, came into the world not as a material being; Christ appeared in the likeness of human flesh, to paraphrase the apostle Paul. Jesus wasn't really a human being, he only seemed to be a human being; he only seemed to be consisting of flesh, and bone, and blood. The Marcionites, in other words, were docetic. They said that Jesus was God, but he wasn't human. They had books that authorized their view; they took the writings of the apostle Paul, and they had something like our Gospel of Luke—books that they said showed that Christ was God, and not human, and that the Jewish God, in fact, was not the God of Jesus or Paul.

It's easy to contrast the Marcionites and the Ebionites. The Ebionites were Jewish; the Marcionites were anti-Jewish. The Ebionites were monotheist; the Marcionites were ditheist. The Ebionites were against Paul; the Marcionites were for Paul. The Ebionites said Christ was man, but not God; the Marcionites said Christ was God and not man. You can simply go through their beliefs and line them up against each other. Both of them claimed to be right; both of them had books that supported their views; both of them said their views were the views of Jesus himself; and both groups ended up being declared heretical. Both groups were condemned by the group that emerged as victorious in the struggle to determine what Christians ought to believe and how they ought to worship. It was the group that condemned both of these other groups that ended up giving us the scriptures that are accepted as canonical today, as we'll see in our final lecture.

To sum up, Christianity became a text-based religion because it invoked the need for proper belief; and proper belief required proper knowledge; and proper knowledge required established authorities; and authorities that are written, in theory, are more certain than those that are merely spoken, because written sources provide their words in permanent form, in form that is available to anybody with eyes to see.

Lecture Eleven
The Importance of Interpretation

Scope: Even as Christians began to agree on which books were to be accepted as authoritative, in the process of forming a new canon of Scripture, they were confronted with a basic problem: It is one thing to *have* a book that is considered authoritative, but it is another thing to *interpret* the book. And as Christians have long realized, interpretations of authoritative books vary widely, sometimes radically, with different readers claiming that the book means different things.

In this lecture, we will consider the ways early Christians tried to interpret their authoritative texts, taking special note of the movement among numerous Christian readers to take their texts not just literally but also figuratively. But figurative readings—though used by nearly all early Christians—created a problem: If a text means something other than what it says, how can you control its interpretation to prevent a "false teacher" from using it to his own ends?

Outline

I. We saw in the previous lecture that Christianity from the outset was a text-based religion and that Christians, therefore, had to decide which books were to be considered sacred. But knowing which books are sacred provides no guarantee that everyone will agree on what to believe.

    A. The problem is that different interpreters can interpret the same book in different ways.

        1. This is obvious even today, given that different Christians from different churches interpret the New Testament in radically different ways.

        2. And this is true not just of the New Testament or other sacred books but of all books altogether. Just consider the wide-ranging interpretations of Shakespeare or the American Constitution!

3. The problem is that written texts are never self-interpreting. They always require human beings to interpret them, and humans have different views, beliefs, values, priorities, worldviews, ideas, and so on—and all these things affect how one reads a text; thus, the same text can mean different things to different people.

B. For early Christians to ensure that the "right" beliefs would be held, they had to do more than choose which books were authoritative; they also had to determine how these books were to be interpreted.

II. The problem was well recognized in the early centuries of Christianity, as different groups interpreted the sacred Scriptures in radically different ways.

A. The famous "heretic" Marcion, for example, used a literal interpretation to discredit the writings of the Hebrew Scriptures, which for other Christians were the sacred "Old Testament."

1. Marcion based his views on the writings of Paul, who differentiated between the Law and the Gospel.

2. For Marcion, this was an absolute distinction, to the point that the God who gave the Law to the Jews was obviously not the same God who provided salvation from the Law through Jesus.

3. Marcion wrote a book called the *Antitheses* (meaning "contrary statements"), in which he showed that the teachings of the Jewish Bible contradicted the teachings of Jesus.

4. His conclusion was that it was the Gospel of Jesus, as proclaimed by Paul, that was to be observed; the Jewish Bible was not to be accepted as Christian Scripture.

B. Other allegedly false teachers, such as the Gnostics, did not opt for a literal interpretation of texts but moved into highly figurative modes of interpretation.

1. Gnostics maintained that this world was an evil place in which portions of the divine (our inner selves) had come to be trapped in matter (our bodies). The point of their religion was to provide escape by transmitting the "knowledge" (*gnosis*) that is necessary to escape our imprisonment.

2. For Gnostics, there are three kinds of people in the world: pure animals that have no afterlife; people (such as normal

Christians) who can have faith and do good works, and will have an afterlife as a reward; and elite Christians (Gnostics) who had a heavenly pre-existence. When they are set free by the "saving knowledge" they will return to the realm whence they came.

3. Behind the idea of salvation by knowledge lay a set of complicated myths that explained how this world and the world of the divine beings came into existence.

4. One of these myths talks about an unknowable God; we cannot know him because our knowledge is restricted to our senses and this God is immaterial.

5. Divine beings called Aeons emanated from this God; the twelfth divine being was Sophia (wisdom) who tried to understand the divine realm and overreached her grasp; she fell from the divine world and in her fall, conceived an imperfect offspring, the creator of the material world.

6. This demiurge declared he was the only God (the God of the Old Testament). He and his minions split up his mother, Sophia, into a million pieces, which became entrapped in human bodies. Thus, some humans have a "divine spark" of Sophia in them.

7. Sophia longs to be set free and in order for this to happen the people with the "divine spark" of Sophia in them need to know how they came to be on Earth and how they can return to the divine world they came from.

8. Gnostics believed they had the power to receive this sacred knowledge which could come only from a being from the divine world, i.e.: Christ

9. The Gospel of John portrays Jesus as a divine being who comes to earth to reveal the divine truth necessary for salvation, a view that was very amenable to Gnostics.

10. Orthodox Christians opposed the Gnostic interpretation of John, just as they opposed Gnostic interpretations more broadly, because Gnostics were inclined *not* to accept the literal understanding of the Scriptures. They believed that just as Sophia is trapped within the body, so too, truth is entrapped beneath the literal words of a text.

11. Some of the Gnostics' interpretations of Scripture were used to support their myths. For example, some Gnostics believed

that there were 30 divine beings in the divine realm, who had all emanated from the one true God. Evidence came in the circumstance that Jesus started his ministry when he was 30 years old.

12. The idea that the 12th divine being was the one whose fall from the divine realm is what led to the creation of this miserable material world was shown by the fact that it was Jesus' 12th disciple, Judas Iscariot, who betrayed him.

13. Church fathers responding to this kind of teaching stressed that the Gnostic figurative interpretations of Scripture had nothing to do with their literal meanings.

14. In an effective image used by the church father Irenaeus, the Gnostic interpretations of Scripture are like someone taking a gorgeous mosaic of a king, rearranging its stones into the image of a dog, and claiming that's what the artist had in mind all along.

C. Even proto-orthodox church leaders used figurative modes of interpretation when it suited them, however.

1. The church father Barnabas, for example, interpreted the laws of Jews, including circumcision, Sabbath observance, and kosher food laws, as symbolic statements of what people should believe and how people should behave, rather than as literal laws to be followed.

2. Thus, even though proto-orthodox Christians emphasized the need to interpret texts literally in order to know what God meant to teach them, they, too, used figurative modes of interpretation when it suited their purposes.

D. Despite this ambivalence on the proper approach to interpretation, it can be said that for most proto-orthodox leaders, the literal mode of interpretation was to be given preference to the symbolic in trying to decide what the Scriptures really mean.

III. The debates over interpretation continued for centuries.

A. Throughout most of Christian history, figurative interpretations were sanctioned and encouraged.

B. Eventually, with the Reformation and the Enlightenment, the literal approach to interpretation came to be championed and privileged, until today, when it seems simply like the "commonsensical" way to read texts.

C. But we should always remember that "common" sense simply means the sense shared by the majority of persons at any given time. Commonsense views are not necessarily true; they are simply widely shared.

IV. In sum, there were wide debates in the early church over how to interpret the texts of Scripture. Although these debates may have subsided, their significance has not: Christians continue to disagree in fundamental ways about what their sacred texts teach about what to believe and how to live.

Essential Reading:

Bart D. Ehrman, *The Orthodox Corruption of Scripture*, chapter 1.

Karlfried Froehlich, *Biblical Interpretation in the Early Church*.

Supplementary Reading:

Water Bauer, *Orthodoxy and Heresy in Earliest Christianity*.

Robert M. Grant and David Tracy, *A Short History of the Interpretation of the Bible*.

Questions to Consider:

1. Are there any situations today in which a "non-literal" reading of a text is to be preferred over a literal one?

2. In your judgment, if church fathers disallowed a figurative interpretation of Scripture for the Gnostics, how could they deny the merit of Marcion's claim that when read literally, the texts of the Jewish Scriptures seem to present a God who is different from the God of Jesus?

Lecture Eleven—Transcript
The Importance of Interpretation

We saw in the previous lecture that Christianity, from the outset, was a text-based religion, and that Christians, therefore, had to decide which books were sacred. But knowing which books are sacred provides no guarantee that everyone will agree on what to believe. The problem is that different interpreters can interpret the same book in different ways. This is obvious, even today, given the fact that different Christians from different churches interpret the New Testament in radically different ways. The Southern Baptists interpret the New Testament quite differently from the Catholics; the Lutherans interpret it differently from the Mormons; the Episcopalians, from the Seventh Day Adventists. This is true not just of the New Testament or other sacred books, but of all books altogether—just consider the wide-ranging interpretations of Shakespeare or the American Constitution.

The problem is that written texts are never self-interpreting. They always require human beings to interpret them; and human beings have different views, beliefs, values, priorities, worldviews, ideas, and so on. And all these things affect how one reads a text. Thus, the same text can mean different things to different people. For early Christians to ensure that the right beliefs would be held, they had to do more than choose which books were authoritative. They also had to determine how these books were to be interpreted. The problem was well recognized in the early centuries of Christianity, as different groups interpreted the same scriptures in radically different ways.

The famous heretic Marcion, for example, whom I talked about in the previous lecture, used a literal interpretation to discredit the writings of the Hebrew scriptures, which for other Christians were the sacred Old Testament. If you remember, Marcion believed that the Jewish scriptures were the scriptures of the Jewish God, who had created the world and called Israel to be his people. But these scriptures were not to be the scriptures of the Christians because the Christians worshipped the other God, the God who had sent Jesus into the world to save Christians from the God of wrath described in the Old Testament. Marcion had, as his sacred books, something like our Gospel of Luke and something like our letters of Paul. In fact, he had all of our letters of Paul, except for the Pastoral Epistles, First and Second Timothy, and Titus. That was his canon of scripture—the letters of Paul and something like our Gospel of Luke. He nonetheless read the Old

Testament; he read the Old Testament precisely because he wanted his understanding of the Old Testament to show that the God of the Old Testament could not be the God of Jesus. To show this, Marcion read the Old Testament in a very literalistic way, to show that the God of wrath that the Old Testament portrays simply could not be the God proclaimed by Paul and Jesus before him.

One of Marcion's most famous writings was a book called *The Antitheses*. The word *antithesis* means "contrary statements." In this book, *The Antitheses*, Marcion tried to show that a literal reading of the Old Testament, when compared with a literal reading of the writings of Paul and the teachings of Jesus, contradicted one another. They stand in contrary relationship to one another; they are antithetical. This showed that the God of the Old Testament could not be the God of Jesus. Let me give you a couple of examples. We don't actually have *The Antitheses* anymore; we don't have Marcion's writing. We have it only as it was quoted by some of the church fathers, but there are places where we're able to reconstruct what Marcion's antithesis said, and, thereby, reconstruct what he had to say about the relationship of the Hebrew Bible to the teachings of Jesus and Paul.

Marcion maintained that the God of the Old Testament simply could not be the same God Jesus talked about. For example, the God of the Old Testament, after the Exodus, tells the children of Israel to go into the Promised Land and to take it for themselves. The problem was, of course, that somebody already lived in the Promised Land. What were the Israelites to do about that? According to the book of Joshua, they were to kill the people in the Promised Land. And so in the famous story of the Battle of Jericho, we're told that God instructed Joshua to have the people of Israel march around the city of Jericho that was inhabited by the Canaanites. They're to march around the city once a day for seven days; and on the seventh day, they're to march around the city seven times, and then to blow their trumpets, and then the walls of Jericho will fall down. When the walls of Jericho fall, the children of Israel are to invade the city, attack it, and murder every man, woman, and child in the city. Joshua does so at the commandment of God. They destroy all the inhabitants of Jericho, and Marcion asks, "Is this the same God who says, 'Love your enemy?' Is this the same God who says, 'If somebody strikes on you the right cheek, turn to him the other also?' Is this the same God who says, 'Pray for those who persecute you?'" Jesus taught about a God of love and mercy and forgiveness. The God of the Battle of Jericho is anything but a God of love, mercy, and forgiveness. These simply cannot be the same God, based on a literal interpretation of the Jewish scriptures.

Take a second example: in the Hebrew Bible, there's a passage in the book of Kings about the prophet Elijah. Elijah is walking by a group of boys, and these boys start making fun of him. Elijah, apparently, was going bald, and these boys call out, "Baldy! Baldy!" This irritates the prophet of God who calls God's wrath down upon these children, and there emerges from a nearby forest two she-bears who come up against the boys and attack them and maul 46 of them. Is this the same God who said, "Let the little children come unto me?" Surely, it's a different God. The God of the Old Testament cannot be the God of Jesus, the God of Paul.

Marcion's conclusion was what he considered to be a straightforward, literal interpretation of the Old Testament, and shows that the Gospel of Jesus, especially as it was proclaimed by Paul, was not the same as the Law and the Gospel proclaimed in the Old Testament. The Jewish Bible, in other words, is not to be accepted as Christian scripture. Marcion had a canon of a scripture. He had a collection of sacred books that he thought were authoritative: Luke and ten letters of Paul, with no Old Testament. The Old Testament is the scripture of the Jews; it's not the scripture of the Christians.

This view, of course, did not end up winning out. This view ended up losing to the Christians who insisted that the Jewish heritage is important to hold on to. Christians insisted that Jesus himself was Jewish, that he was a Jewish teacher who taught the true meaning of the Jewish Law. Christians eventually held on to the Old Testament, but they had to interpret the Old Testament in light of their Christian faith. And so, eventually, Christians came to teach that the Old Testament and the New Testament gods are, in fact, the same God, and can be reconciled with one another over the teachings of Marcion.

Marcion's views were not the only ones that lost out. There were a large number of various Christian groups in the 2nd, and 3rd, and 4th centuries that held views that eventually came to be eliminated by the victorious party. I mentioned in the previous lecture that it's difficult to define the terms *orthodoxy* and *heresy* because everybody thinks that they hold the right beliefs; in other words, everybody thinks that they are orthodox. Historians continue to use these terms, however, not in their etymological sense to indicate which group was right and which group was wrong. In other words, when historians talk about the orthodox form of Christianity, they're not saying the view that was right, because historians have no access to which view is right; historians have no access to whether there's only one god or two gods or 30 gods or something else. Historians can only describe what happened in history.

One of the things that happened in history is that one group of Christians ended up winning the battles over correct belief. This group that ended up winning the battles for correct belief decided which books to include in the New Testament, and decided what Christians were to believe for all time. They wrote the Christian creeds that have come down to us today. This victorious party, the group that emerged from the conflicts as victorious, the historians call the Orthodox Party—not because they think this group necessarily was right in all of its views, but because this group was the one that was able to determine what the right beliefs are for Christians for all time. The Orthodox Party opposed Marcion; it also opposed the Ebionites; and it opposed another group that I've referred to in previous lectures, a group known as the Gnostics.

The Gnostics are a wide-ranging group of religious persons who subscribe to a range of religious beliefs and practices. There were a number of different Gnostic groups; their views were not necessarily compatible with one another, but there are certain things that all of these groups that scholars call Gnostic had in common. All of these Gnostic groups agreed that the world that we live in is an evil material place that needs to be transcended by the spirits that have been entrapped here. The Gnostics are called *Gnostic* from the Greek word *gnosis*. Gnosis is a Greek word that means "knowledge." Gnostic groups insisted that correct knowledge is the way of salvation. One needs to have the knowledge of who one really is in order to escape this material world.

The idea is that people are trapped in this world; at least, some people are trapped in this world. Some Gnostics maintain, in fact, that there are three kinds of persons in the world. There are some people in this world who are pure animals, like my neighbor. These are people who are simply like mosquitoes, and gnats, and cats, and rats, and other animals—when they die, that's it. That's the end of their existence. They exist no longer. That's one group of person. There's a second group of person for the Gnostics (for some Gnostics) who are a group of people who actually can have an afterlife. These are people who can have faith, and do good works and, as a reward, God will give them an afterlife in Heaven. This will be a good existence after this life. But there's a third group—and by the way, that second group is what would be the normal Christians, the ordinary

Christians—but Gnostics insisted there was a third group of insiders, of elite Christians who have the true knowledge of the faith. These are the Gnostics themselves; these Gnostics maintain that they, in fact, had a preexistence. They are entrapped spirits entrapped in the body; that they can be set free from the body when they acquire the correct *gnosis*, the correct knowledge of existence. When they're set free by the saving knowledge, they can return, then, to the realm whence they came. These spirits preexisted in a Heavenly existence, and they came into this world and were trapped here; but if they return, they'll have glorious afterlife, living in the world of God himself.

How did Gnostics try to explain, though, how the spirits came to be entrapped in this world? Different Gnostic groups had different myths that they used to explain the entrapment of divine sparks in this world. There were a range of Gnostic myths. Different groups had different mythologies, and part of the complication of studying Gnosticism is trying to correlate these various myths with one another. I won't be able to explain all of the various Gnostic myths, but I can give you an example of a kind of Gnostic myth that can explain how it is people came to be entrapped here; how sparks came to be entrapped in this material world.

According to one of the Gnostic myths, the way it happened was this. I should say, in broad outline, this myth is comparable to other Gnostic myths; the details differ significantly, but this is a common type of Gnostic myth. According to one form of the Gnostic myth, in the beginning there was God, who was a truly spiritual being, and completely spiritual, and he was the only thing in existence. Completely spiritual, with nothing material about him, this God is not only the unknown God, he's a God far beyond our knowledge; he's an unknowable God. God is not only unknown, he's unknowable. Why unknowable? Well, because we know things only through our senses. We may think that we have thoughts that are unconnected with our sense experience, but in fact, everything that we think is somehow connected to one of our senses; it's connected to something that we've seen, or heard, or felt, or smelled. Our various senses are what inform our thoughts. But this God is immaterial, and our senses recognize only what's material. This God, therefore, is not only unknown to us; he cannot be known—he's unknowable. I guess as I should say, that as often happens even today, when you have some Christians that will say something like, "God is far beyond what we can think or imagine," and then they start telling you his characteristics, which is, of course, an irony, since, if he's beyond what you can know, then you can't know. That's comparable to what happens with the Gnostics. They indicate that there is this unknowable God, and then they start telling you about him.

This unknowable God, in eternity past, had certain emanations that came forth from him, which were also divine beings. This God did have certain characteristics. This God, for example, was alive; he had life. And so, life itself becomes an entity, a divine being. This God was eternal, so eternality becomes a divine being. This God was all light, no darkness, and so light becomes a divine being. From this God there emanates other divine beings, substances. In one form of the Gnostic myth, these other divine beings emanate out in pairs. There end up being several sets of pairs, in fact, three sets of pairs. First, eight divine beings that are sometimes called Eons— these emanations from the one, true God are called Eons; they're the first eight. Then there's another set of 10 as some of the Eons themselves emanated other divine beings. There are first eight, then 1, and then 12—a total of 30 divine beings, emanations from the one true God.

In one of these Gnostic myths, the twelfth of the 12 divine beings was a divine being called Sofia, "wisdom"—*sofia* is the Greek word for "wisdom." Wisdom wanted to understand the entire divine realm, but in so doing, she overreached her grasp. She wasn't designed to understand the entire divine realm, even though she was called Wisdom. She overreached her grasp and she fell from the divine realm. In her fall, she conceived another emanation, but she fell apart from her consort. All the emanations were in pairs, so that every new emanation came from a previous pairing. She, though, conceives by herself without her partner, so that her offspring is imperfect and partial. This imperfect being that comes into existence with the fall of Sofia is, in fact, the creator of the material world. This demiurge, this maker, makes the material world and declares that he is the only God who exists: "I alone am God and there is no other besides me." That may sound familiar to you. Those are the words of the God of the Old Testament in the book of Isaiah. "I alone am God." This demiurge, this false offspring of Sophia, misunderstood his own existence and thought that he was the only God—the only God that mattered, that is, because he did know about Sofia as a competitor. This God and his minions end up entrapping his mother, Sofia; they create the material world as a place of imprisonment for Sofia. They divide his mother, Sofia, into a million pieces and entrap her in this world in human bodies.

Some humans, then, have a spark of the divine within them, a spark of Sofia that is longing to be set free. How can the spark of Sophia be set free? Only by learning how it is she got here. There are people with the spark of the divine within, and they need to come to know how they came to be here, where they came from, and how they can return. If they receive this kind of personal knowledge of who they really are, then they can escape their entrapment in this material world.

Gnostics, then, give this secret knowledge, this knowledge of the truth of one's real being. People who are Gnostic, then, the Gnostics themselves, receive this knowledge, and upon the death of their body, they can return to the heavenly realm whence they came. Not everybody is a Gnostic, not everybody has this spark within; only some people have the spark within. How, though, are they supposed to get the knowledge? They can't get the knowledge simply by looking around the world and thinking hard about it, and figuring it all out, because that involves using your sense experience. The only way that one can receive the knowledge of the "real" world, the divine realm, is if a figure from the divine realm comes down and reveals the secret knowledge. In these Gnostic systems, Christ is a divine being who comes from the divine realm to reveal the secret knowledge that's necessary for salvation. Once you learn that knowledge, then you can be set free. "You shall know the truth, and the truth shall make you free," as it says in the Gospel of John, a Gospel much liked by many Gnostic groups, because the Gospel of John portrays Jesus as a divine being, who comes to earth to reveal the truth necessary for salvation. This is very amenable to Gnostic views.

The Orthodox people, of course, opposed the Gnostic interpretation of John as they opposed Gnostic interpretations more broadly, of various scriptures, because the Gnostics were particularly inclined not to accept the literal surface understanding of the scriptures. This is where they differed significantly from Marcion. Gnostics understood that, just as Sofia is entrapped within the body, so too, true knowledge is entrapped in the literal words of the text. One needs to go below the literal words to see the true spiritual meaning if one is to understand the sacred writings.

In a number of instances, they came up with very interesting interpretations of scriptural text that others thought were, in fact, outlandish—others who were non-Gnostic. For example, some Gnostics believed, as I've pointed out, that there were 30 divine beings in the divine realm—a set of eight, a set of 10, and a set of 12. Evidence that there are 30 divine beings, for some Gnostics, came in the circumstance that according to the Gospel of Luke, Jesus began his ministry when he was 30 years old. Why 30 years old? Because it's a symbolic representation of the divine *Aeon*, of the divine beings. The idea that the twelfth of the Duodecad—the twelfth of the group of 12, Sofia—was the one that fell from the divine realm leading to this miserable material world was shown by the fact that it was Jesus' twelfth disciple, Judas Iscariot, who betrayed him. The twelfth disciple betrayed him—that's, in fact, a symbolic representation of the fall of Sofia in the divine realm.

Gnostics had symbolic interpretations of the writing scripture. They wouldn't accept the literal interpretations, which made them very difficult to argue with, because it was impossible to point to a passage of scripture and say, "See, you're wrong because the text says this." Because Gnostics would say, "Well, yeah, it says this on the surface, but what it really means is this." "Yeah, but it says that." "It doesn't matter what it says, this is what it means." It's very difficult to argue with somebody like that, as it's difficult to argue with a Gnostic, generally, because a Gnostic is someone who has knowledge; and if you're not a Gnostic, you don't have knowledge; and so if you disagree, it's simply because you're ignorant. "Yes, but that's not right." "That's what you think because you're ignorant; I have knowledge." It's very difficult to argue with that sort of view.

The church fathers who were of the Orthodox persuasion—in other words, the church fathers whose views ended up winning out—argued against the Gnostics and, as it turns out, argued quite effectively. In other words, they convinced more people so that they ended up winning. They argued that these kinds of figurative interpretations were wrong because these Gnostic figurative readings of scripture had nothing to do with the literal meanings of the text. There's an effective image used by one of the church fathers, a church father named Irenaeus. Irenaeus said that the Gnostics interpreting scriptures are like somebody who takes a gorgeous mosaic of a king—a mosaic made out of colored stones—and rearranges the colored stones so that now they take on the appearance of a mongrel dog; and then they claim that that's what the artist had in mind all along. That's what the Gnostics do; they take the literal meaning of the text, and they rearrange things so that it ends up looking completely unlike what it originally looked like. The church fathers, the Orthodox Church fathers, argued against these kinds of figurative interpretations of scripture.

What's striking to historians, though, is that even Orthodox Church leaders used figurative modes of interpretation when it suited their own purposes. The church father Tertullian, for example, argues for a literal interpretation of the text, but whenever it suits his purposes, can talk about a symbolic meaning of the text. Before him, the church father Barnabas interpreted the laws of the Jews found in the Jewish scripture as having symbolic meaning—laws including things such as the law of circumcision. He thought the law of circumcision didn't really mean that you should cut the foreskin of your baby boys. No, it was a symbolic statement that you should believe in the cross of Christ. Why the cross of Christ, you ask? It's a little complicated. What Barnabas says is that the father of the Jews, Abraham, was the first to circumcise, and he circumcised 318 of his servants prior to leading them off to war, according to the book of Genesis. Why 318, asks Barnabas? Because this is a symbolic number; in Greek, when you write out the number 318, you use letters of the alphabet, the letters are Tao, Iota, Eta. Tao looks like our "T"—it's in the form of a cross. Iota and Eta are the first two letters of the name *Jesus* and so the circumcision of 318 is actually the cross of Jesus. Barnabas concludes by saying, "No one has ever learned a better lesson from me." And I'm sure he's right. He interpreted the Sabbath laws symbolically, the kosher food laws symbolically. The church fathers, when it suited their purposes, could interpret the scriptures symbolically rather than literally. Even so, the Orthodox Christians, who eventually won out in these battles, stress that the texts are primarily needed to be interpreted literally, in order to know what God meant to teach by them; and only then could they be interpreted following figurative modes of interpretation. But you couldn't use figurative modes of interpretation to overturn literal interpretation.

Despite the somewhat ambivalence on the issue, it can be said that for most Orthodox leaders, the literal mode of interpretation was to be given preference to the symbolic, in trying to decide what it is the scriptures really mean. These debates over how to interpret continued on for centuries. Throughout most of Christian history, to the discomfort of many Christians today, figurative interpretations were both sanctioned and encouraged. For most of Christian history, symbolic interpretations of scripture had been completely acceptable, even encouraged. Eventually, though, with the Reformation and the Enlightenment, the literal approach to interpretation came to be championed and privileged, so that today, it simply seems like the commonsensical way to read a text; you read a text literally. We need to remember, though, that this is common sense because of what *common sense* means. Common sense means a sense that is shared by the majority of people at any given time. Commonsense views are not necessarily true; they're simply widely shared. For much of Christian history, common sense indicated that scriptures are to be read symbolically, especially with the Reformation, when Martin Luther insisted that the text itself is the final authority in all matters of theology. He had to insist on a literal interpretation of the text because, otherwise, a symbolic interpretation could lead to other views. The insistence in the Reformation of *sola scriptura*— "scripture alone"—as the guide to true theology, led to an insistence on the literal interpretation of the text, so much so that people in the modern world read text almost always literally rather than symbolically.

In sum, there were wide debates in the early Church over how to interpret the text to scripture. Although these debates have subsided by now, their significance has not. Christians continue to disagree, in fundamental ways, about the way their sacred texts teach, about what to believe, and how to live.

Lecture Twelve

When Did the Canon Get Finalized?

Scope: In our concluding lecture, we will ask how, why, and when the canon of the New Testament came to be finalized so that we ended up with 27 books, and just these 27 books, no more and no fewer. Is it true, as stated in some popular fiction, that the 4th-century emperor Constantine made the decision about which books were to be included? Who did make the decision, and on what grounds?

In the course of this concluding lecture, we will consider some of the books that nearly made it into the New Testament but were finally excluded, such as the Apocalypse of Peter, as well as some books that did make it in but nearly did not, such as the Apocalypse of John.

Outline

I. Despite the fact that different Christians could interpret books in different ways, it became important to the proto-orthodox Christians to know which books were Scripture.

  A. In part, this was because they wanted to differentiate themselves from Jews, who also had a collection of sacred books.

  B. But in larger part, it was because there were competing understandings of the faith, each claiming "apostolic" authority for its views.

  C. Proto-orthodox Christians then wanted to know which books should be included in a sacred canon of Scripture and which could be safely excluded.

  D. The debates over which books to include and exclude were long and drawn out; the matter was not decided, in fact, for centuries.

II. There were some books that were not, ultimately, included in the New Testament that were, at one time or another, by one proto-orthodox group or another, considered Scripture.

  A. This is true, for example, of the Gospel of Peter, a fragment of which was discovered at the end of the 19th century.

1. We've known about the Gospel of Peter for centuries because it was written about by Eusebius in the 4th century, but we didn't have the actual book until it was discovered in the 1860s.
2. The story that Eusebius tells is interesting because it describes a period of church history that we know little about.
3. Eusebius is sometimes called "the father of church history," because he is the first church father to write a history of the church from the days of Jesus to Eusebius' own time at the beginning of the 4th century.
4. Eusebius quotes at length a number of documents that no longer survive; among them is the story of the Gospel of Peter.
5. Eusebius tells a story about Serapian, a late 2nd century church father, who was a bishop of Antioch in Syria.
6. Serapian sanctioned the use of the Gospel of Peter by a church in Rhossus. But people told him that the Gospel of Peter contained docetic Christology.
7. When Serapian read the book, he realized that some passages could be interpreted docetically and forbad its use. Thus, the Gospel of Peter came to be excluded from the canon and disappeared.
8. The book as we have it, in any event, is very interesting, because it is the only early Gospel to give an actual account of what happened at Jesus' resurrection.
B. Another book allegedly by Peter, the so-called Apocalypse of Peter, was considered even more broadly to be part of Scripture up until the 4th century.
   1. This book, too, was unavailable to us until the end of the 19th century.
   2. This book is also very interesting, because it is the first surviving Christian account of someone being given a guided tour of heaven and hell, as Christ shows Peter the realms of the blessed and the damned.
   3. Eventually, it too, however, was ruled out of court as containing too literalistic an understanding of the afterlife.

III. There were other books that came to be included in the New Testament that were, for many years, under a cloud of suspicion.

A. The Letter to the Hebrews, for example, was considered non-canonical by a large number of proto-orthodox Christians who did not think it was "apostolic." Not until it was accepted as authored by the apostle Paul (it never claims to be) was it received into the canon.

B. Even more problematic was the Book of Revelation.

    1. Part of the problem was uncertainty over the identity of its author.

    2. It claims to be written by John, but which "John" is not known. Its writing style is quite different from the style of the Gospel of John.

    3. Scholars continue to believe to this day that the author of the Gospel of John and the author of the Revelation of John are not the same person.

    4. Eventually some Christians argued that Revelation should not be included in the canon because its literal portrayal of a 1,000-year reign of Christ after a bloody tribulation on Earth was too naively literalistic an understanding of what would happen at the end of time.

IV. Despite the uncertainties, there was a clear movement to establish a canon of Scripture from the earliest days of Christianity.

    A. At the outset, of course, the Jewish Bible was accepted as authoritative (even by Jesus himself).

    B. Before the end of the New Testament period, the sayings of Jesus were considered among Christians to be at least as authoritative as the teachings of the Jewish Scriptures (for example, 1 Timothy 5:18).

    C. Moreover, the writings of Jesus' apostles were sometimes granted scriptural standing, even before the New Testament period was over (cf. 2 Peter 3:16).

V. Debates over which books to include, however, lasted for centuries.

    A. We know of these debates because several lists of books considered to be scriptural have survived from early Christianity, as for example, Eusebius' list of books.

        1. In the 18th century, another list of books was discovered by an Italian scholar named Muratori. The so-called "Muratorian Canon" is a list of books probably made at the end of the 2nd century in Rome by an anonymous Christian author, who apparently considered them to be scriptural.

    2. The author of the Muratorian Canon accepts 22 of the books that came to be included in the New Testament, but does not accept the book of Hebrews, James, 1 and 2 Peter, or 3 John.

    3. He accepts the Apocalypse of Peter and the Wisdom of Solomon, as part of the canon, and rejects other books, including The Shepherd of Hermas because he believed it was not written in apostolic times.

B. Throughout this period, different Christians argued for the canonicity of a variety of books, based largely on four criteria.

    1. A book had to be ancient (written near the time of Jesus).

    2. It had to be by an apostle (or a companion of the apostles).

    3. It had to be widely used throughout the church.

    4. Most especially, it had to be "orthodox" (communicating the "right teaching").

C. To the surprise of many people today, the first Christian of record to maintain that the New Testament was to consist of the 27 books accepted today was the Alexandrian bishop Athanasius in A.D. 367—some 300 years after most of these books had been written!

D. Even after Athanasius's day, there continued to be disputes, until the matter was more or less resolved for most Christians around the 5th century.

E. There was no ecumenical church council that made this decision (although some local councils ratified the list on occasion). Instead, it was a matter of popular opinion, which affected, of course, which books were actually copied over time.

    1. Churches and individuals were most interested in having copies of the Scripture; thus, these were the books that were reproduced more often (some of them more frequently than others; Mark, for example, was not copied nearly as often as John).

    2. Other books disappeared from the scene not because there were massive book burnings, but simply because no one saw the need to copy them, and the surviving copies were lost, worn out, destroyed, or simply thrown away.

VI. With the invention of the printing press, there was no longer any question about which books would be included in the New Testament, because the same 27 books in the same sequence were copied time after time.

VII. Thus, we have our New Testament today, the collection of books that has proved more significant for the history and culture of Western civilization than any other, without rival in the West for its social and religious importance.

Essential Reading:

Bart D. Ehrman, *Lost Christianities: The Battles for Scripture and the Faiths We Never Knew.*

———, *The New Testament: A Historical Introduction to the Early Christian Writings*, chapter 1.

Supplementary Reading:

Harry Gamble, *The New Testament Canon: Its Making and Meaning.*

Bruce M. Metzger, *The Canon of the New Testament: Its Origin, Development, and Significance.*

Questions to Consider:

1. How might Christianity have been different if the Gospel of Peter or the Apocalypse of Peter had made it into the New Testament? Of if the Book of Revelation had not?

2. In your opinion, should the canon of the New Testament remain theoretically open? That is to say, should the Christian Church have the right to decide to exclude some books or to add others to the canon?

Lecture Twelve—Transcript
When Did the Canon Get Finalized?

Despite the fact that different Christians could interpret books in different ways, it became important to the Orthodox Christians to know which books were scripture. In part, this was because they wanted to differentiate themselves from Jews, who also had a collection of sacred books. So with the passing of time, as Christianity began to separate itself more and more from its mother religion, Judaism, the Christians wanted to differentiate themselves not only in what they believed and how they practiced, but also in what books they had. They wanted their own sacred scriptures, not necessarily to contradict those of the Jews, but to show why they were distinctively Christian. That's one reason for Christians collecting their own books, distinctively Christian books, in their own canon of scripture, the New Testament. But another reason, and probably the primary reason for Christians developing a canon of scripture, is because there were competing understandings of the faith, each of them claiming apostolic authority for its views, as we have seen. There were a variety of groups that have a variety of scriptures that authorized a variety of beliefs.

Christians, then, had to decide which books would be included in their canon of scripture, so that they would know what to believe and how to practice their religion. The debates over which books to include in the canon and which to exclude were long and drawn-out. The matter, in fact, was not decided for centuries. This comes as a surprise to many of my students, who simply think that the New Testament appeared one day soon after Jesus died. In fact, not only were the books written decades after Jesus' death, but they weren't considered scripture for a long time after that, and they weren't collected into a canon for a long time after that. The debate, as I've indicated, went on for centuries.

There were some books that were not, ultimately, included in the New Testament, that at one time or another, by one group or another, were considered scripture—as we've seen, for example, in the case of the Ebionites, with their form of the Gospel of Matthew; the Marcionites, with their form of the Gospel of Luke; or with the Gnostics, who had a variety of texts. The Gnostics didn't limit themselves to interpreting the text, such as the Gospel of John, that came into the canon of the New Testament. The Gnostics had their own writings, as well, many of which they considered scripture. And we've discovered a number of these writings; the most important discovery was made in 1945 near a village called Nag Hammadi,

Egypt. This was the discovery in which the Gospel of Thomas was found, along with 44 other texts that some Gnostics apparently considered to be scriptural, including other Gospels. There was a Gospel of Philip discovered at Nag Hammadi, for example, a Gospel called the Gospel of Truth, and a range of other texts that were related. For example, there were the Gnostic myths, such as the secret book of John; or a book called, *The Origin of the Worlds*. Some Gnostic groups considered these texts to be scripture. Or there were texts discovered earlier in the 19th century that were considered by Gnostic groups to be scripture, including the Gospel of Mary, the only Gospel that we have that claims to be written by a woman.

There were a range of books considered by different groups to be Christian, but even the group that ended up establishing orthodoxy accepted, at one point or another, at one place or another, at one time or another, books that eventually were excluded from the canon of scripture. Let me give you a couple of examples.

One is an example that I've referred to already, the Gospel of Peter. The Gospel of Peter is an interesting case because we've known about the Gospel of Peter for centuries—it was written by the church father Eusebius in the 4th century—even though we didn't have it. This was a case where we knew of the existence of the book that we had lost. We knew about the Gospel of Peter since the time of Eusebius in the 4th century, but we didn't have the book until it was discovered in this archeological find by this French archeological team in the 1860s. When digging up a Christian cemetery in the region of Akhmim, Egypt, they uncovered a tomb of a monk. The tomb was an 8th-century tomb; the monk, apparently, was an 8th-century monk buried in the tomb with a book. The book had several texts in it; one of the four texts in this book was the Gospel of Peter. So this was a case where we discovered a text that we already had known was in existence before.

The story that Eusebius gives of the Gospel of Peter is very interesting for those interested in this understanding of why we got the canon that we got. The story that Eusebius tells is interesting because it's one of these stories where Eusebius gives us information about a period of church history that, otherwise, we're fairly ignorant of. Let me give you a bit of background. Eusebius is sometimes called the Father of Church History. He's called that because he is the first Church father to write a history of the Christians from the beginning until his own day. *Eusebius's Church History*, or *Ecclesiastical History* as it's sometimes called, is in 10 volumes; it was 10 books long. We still have it—it's still available. You can buy it now in any

good used bookstore or online in a good English translation—*Eusebius'*
Church History in 10 books. It deals with Christianity from the days of
Jesus to Eusebius's own time, at the very beginning of the 4th century, to the
time when the Emperor Constantine converted to Christianity, leading
eventually to Christianity becoming the religion of the Empire. Eusebius
chronicles the history of the Church up to that time, and he gives us
information about the Christian Church that, otherwise, we would have no
access to. One of the best parts of Eusebius's book is that he quotes, at
length, a number of documents that no longer survive, so that we're able to
use Eusebius's book to reconstruct writings that are no longer in existence
from the 2nd and 3rd Christian centuries.

Included among his stories, is the story of the Gospel of Peter. The story
that Eusebius tells is of a late-2nd-century church father named Serapian.
Serapian was a bishop of the city of Antioch in Syria. This was a very
important church that he was the bishop of, one of the largest churches of
the 2nd century. Serapian had a good deal of authority. Included in his
jurisdiction, were the churches in the villages and towns surrounding the
very large city of Antioch. On occasion, Serapian would make the rounds,
where he would visit these various village churches to make sure that things
were going alright among the Christians there. As Eusebius tells the story,
Serapian was visiting a church in the village of Rosas. This church in the
village of Rosas, evidently, used as its scripture, text that was read during
their church services, a book called the Gospel of Peter. When Serapian
learned that the Christians of Rosas were reading the Gospel of Peter, he
approved its use in the church, thinking that if Simon Peter the apostle had
written a Gospel, then surely it's acceptable. And so, he sanctioned their use
of the Gospel of Peter.

But when Serapian returned home to Antioch, several people came forward
to inform him that, in fact, this Gospel of Peter was highly suspect
theologically. According to these informers, the Gospel of Peter, in fact,
contained a docetic Christology—in other words, it taught that Jesus wasn't
really a human being, but only seemed to be a human being. He was a
human only in appearance. In other words, according to these informers, the
Gospel of Peter was a heretical Gospel, not a true Gospel. Serapian, then,
acquired a copy of the Gospel of Peter and read it for himself. He realized
that there were some passages in the Gospel of Peter that, in fact, could be
interpreted docetically. So Serapian wrote a letter to the Christians of Rosas
in which he detailed the problematic passages in the Gospel of Peter and
forbad its future use. Eusebius quotes from this letter of Serapian, indicating

that he found this Gospel of Peter to be problematic, but unfortunately, Eusebius does not quote the offending passages.

The reason that's significant is, when they discovered a fragmentary copy of the Gospel of Peter in 1868, it's impossible to know if this Gospel of Peter that they discovered in the monk's tomb is the same Gospel of Peter that Serapian had read, because Serapian's quotations of that Gospel of Peter don't survive in Eusebius's account of the story. It's simply an assumption that this Gospel of Peter that was found is, in fact, the same Gospel of Peter that Serapian refers to. Nonetheless, it appears completely plausible that this is the same book. The reason is that this Gospel that was found in the tomb of the monk claims to be written by Peter, as did the Gospel of Peter that Cyprian read. Moreover, there are passages in this Gospel of Peter that we now have that can be read docetically. I pointed out one when we were talking about the Gospel of Peter. At one point it says that Jesus on the cross was silent, "as if he felt no pain." Now, it's not clear that that verse is docetic, but it certainly could be read docetically, which is exactly what Cyprian said about the Gospel of Peter. He said on the most part it's fine, but there are these passages that could be read docetically, and so he forbad its use. Eventually, then, this book, even though it was accepted by some Orthodox Christians (those in Rosas), eventually it came to be excluded from the canon. Therefore, it just simply disappeared, as people didn't copy it through the ages.

I'll give you a second example, another book allegedly by Peter. This book is called the Apocalypse of Peter, which very interestingly, was also found in the same tomb of the same monk. This monk was buried with a book. It was an anthology, as I've indicated, with four texts in it. One is a fragmentary copy of the Gospel of Peter; the other is a copy of the Apocalypse of Peter. I briefly mentioned this Apocalypse of Peter in an earlier lecture. This Apocalypse of Peter is the first instance we have of a Christian text in which the author is given a guided tour of Heaven and Hell. People are familiar with this literary motif from the writings of Dante, *The Divine Comedy*, but it's important to realize that Dante didn't come up with this idea of somebody taking a tour of Heaven and Hell. This, in fact, has a very long tradition behind it; and this Apocalypse of Peter, which dates from the 2nd century, is certainly is the first instance of this motif that survives.

Peter is talking with Jesus, according to this text, about the fate of souls in the afterlife, and Jesus gives him a tour of the realms of the blessed and the realms of the damned. The tour of the realms of the blessed is a fairly interesting tour because you get to see how people enjoy eternal life; but there are only so many ways you can describe eternal bliss, so it's not as fascinating as the tour of the realms of the damned. You can be very creative, indeed, when you want to describe eternal torment. The Apocalypse of Peter is, in fact, quite detailed and graphic in its descriptions of how people are tortured forever because of their sins. It turns out, according to the Apocalypse of Peter, that people are tortured according to the particular sins that they committed during their lives. For example, people who were habitual liars in the realm of the damned, Peter sees that they are hung by their tongues over eternal flames because they were liars. Those who were habitual adulterers are hung by a different body part over eternal flame, and so it goes. Women who plaited their hair in order to be attractive to men are hung by their hair over eternal flame, and so it goes. People are punished according to the crimes that they committed. This Apocalypse of Peter was very popular in the early Church. We know of some early Church fathers who insisted that the Apocalypse of Peter, rather than the Apocalypse of John, should be included in the New Testament; or that the Apocalypse of Peter, in addition to the Apocalypse of John, should be included in the New Testament. Eventually, though, the Apocalypse of Peter was ruled out of court as containing too literalistic an understanding of what the afterlife involved.

My point up to this stage is that there were several books that were perfectly acceptable to some Orthodox authors, that were unacceptable to others; and there were debates over whether these books should be included in the canon or not. Only one side ended up winning those debates, and so the Gospel of Peter, and the Apocalypse of Peter, and other books similar to them, were excluded. On the other hand, there were several books that were included in the canon of scripture that were subject to considerable debate, that nearly didn't make it in. Let me give you two examples.

The letter to the Hebrews in the New Testament is a difficult letter because it's included among the letters of Paul in the New Testament, and, in fact, was accepted into the New Testament because it was thought that the book of Hebrews was written by Paul. But there were debates from early times about whether Paul wrote the letter to the Hebrews, because it doesn't claim to be written by Paul. Paul's name never occurs in the text of the letter to the Hebrews. In fact, the letter to the Hebrews is not even a letter; it appears to be a sermon. Christians debated for decades and even centuries, concerning whether this letter to the Hebrews could be accepted in scripture—one of the reasons being that it seemed to teach a view that was contrary to other passages that were considered scriptural. One of the things that the Letter to the Hebrews teaches is that if somebody becomes a Christian and then falls away, they have permanently lost their salvation. Hebrews, chapter 6, verse 4, and following: "It is impossible to restore again to repentance those who have once been enlightened, and have tasted the heavenly gift, and shared in the Holy Spirit, and tasted the goodness of the word of the God and the powers of the age to come, and then have fallen away, since on their own, they are crucifying again the son of God and are holding him up to contempt." Once somebody falls away from the faith, they cannot be restored, even if they repent. This seemed to some Christians to be contrary to teachings that, for example, you can find in the writings of Paul. A number of Christians argued that Paul did not write the letter to the Hebrews, which makes perfectly good sense because the book of the Hebrews doesn't claim to be written by Paul. All of Paul's writings begin by Paul claiming himself as the author.

There were debates, then, over who wrote the book of Hebrews, and there have been a large number of theories over the years, over the centuries, about who wrote the book of Hebrews. Was it Barnabas, Paul's companion? Was it Priscilla, the woman apostle? Was it someone else? Was it Luke, the author of Acts? At the end of the day, probably the Church father Origen, is the one who got it right when he said that, "as to who wrote the letter to the Hebrews, God knows." The point being that God only knows. Hebrews, then, was debated for a long time. Eventually, though, Christians came to think broadly that Paul did write Hebrews, and they included it the canon because they thought Paul wrote it, even though scholars today are unanimous in saying that Paul did not write the book of Hebrews, for a large number of reasons.

A second book that had trouble making it in to the canon was the Book of Revelation, which I discussed in a previous lecture. Revelations nearly didn't make it in. There were a number of Christians who thought that the Book of Revelation did not belong in scripture. Part of the debate had to do with who wrote the Book of Revelation. It's an interesting irony that the Book of Revelation claims to be written by somebody named John, whereas the Gospel of John does not claim to be written by somebody named John. The book that does not claim to be written by somebody named John, we call John; and the book that does claim to be written by somebody named John, we don't call John. That's just one of the ironies. Revelation was written by somebody named John and the question was, which John was it? Was it John the disciple? If it was, then it's an apostolic book and should be included, in the opinion of early Christians. If it were written by a different John, then why would you include it? And so, there were debates over this issue.

Some early Christian scholars pointed out that the writing style of Revelation is quite different from the writing style of the Gospel of John, so it could not be by the same author. That opinion continues to be held by scholars today that. Whoever wrote the Gospel of John, did not write the Book of Revelation. That's absolutely clear once you read these books in Greek, because they have a different writing style.

Eventually, some Christians argued that Revelations should not be included in the canon because it has such a literalistic portrayal of a millennium on earth, a literal 1,000-year reign of Christ after a bloody tribulation on earth. Many Christians thought that this portrayal of a literal 1,000-year millennium was too naïve an understanding of what would happen at the ending of time, and so could not be apostolic. These people argued that Revelation should not belong in the canon. Eventually, though, it came to be thought widely that, in fact, John the son of Zebedee did write the Book of Revelation, as well as the Gospel of John, and so the Book of Revelation came to be included, finally, in the canon of scripture.

Despite the uncertainties, there was a clear movement to establish a canon of scripture from the earliest days of Christianity. Now what I want to do is talk about how it evolved—how the debates evolved over which books to include. I should say that at the outset, as I've indicated already, Christians started with a canon of scripture because the Jewish Bible was accepted as authoritative by the earliest Christians, even by Jesus himself. Eventually, though, Christians wanted their own authorities in addition to those of the Hebrew Bible, and Christians very early began to consider other writings to be scriptural. In fact, even before the entire New Testament was written, before all the books of the New Testament were finished, the sayings of Jesus were being considered to be as authoritative as the writings of the Jewish scriptures. Jesus' teachings were being considered as authoritative as the scriptures of the Jews.

Evidence of this comes in First Timothy, chapter 5, verse18. The author of First Timothy, which I've argued probably wasn't Paul but somebody writing in Paul's name, at one point wants to make a point about how ministers ought to be paid for their services. He quotes two passages that he labels scripture. He says, "For as the scripture says, you should not muzzle an ox that's grazing," and "A workman is worthy of his hire." He quotes two sayings. The first saying actually occurs in the Law of Moses, "don't muzzle an ox that's treading." The other saying, though, doesn't occur in the Jewish Bible—it's a saying of Jesus that now occurs in the Gospel of Luke, that "a workman is worthy of his hire." This author calls both quotations scripture, which means this author's considering the sayings of Jesus to be equal to the scriptures of the Jews.

Moreover, not just Jesus' own sayings, but sometimes the writings of Jesus' apostles, were granted scriptural standing even before the New Testament period was over. Evidence comes from a passage that I've quoted earlier, Second Peter, chapter 3, verse 16, where the author of Second Peter—this is probably pseudonymous, not Peter himself, writing sometime around the year 120 or so—this author says that, "False teachers have taken the writings of Paul and they've misconstrued them, they've twisted their meaning, as they have with rest of the scriptures," which means he's considering the writings of Paul to be equal with the writings of scripture, the writings of the Hebrew Bible. Even before the end of the New Testament period, we have evidence that Christians are accepting the teachings of Jesus and the writings of his apostles as, in some sense, being scriptural. This leads, of course, to a bipartite canon—Jesus, on the one hand, and the Gospels; and the writings of his apostles, on the other. You have a two-part canon, the Gospels and the other writings.

The debates over which books to include in scripture—even though there was a tendency to accept certain books as scripture—continued on for centuries. We know of this debate because there survived, from early Christianity, several lists of books that authors considered to be scriptural. For example, Eusebius gives a list of books that he considers to be scripture. Moreover, there was discovered in the early 18th century, a list of books that was considered to be scripture by its anonymous author. This list of books, discovered in the early 18th century, was discovered by a guy named Muratori—he was an Italian scholar—and so this list is sometimes called the Muratorian Canon, the Muratorian collection of books. People debate when this thing was made, but the common opinion is that the Muratorian Canon is a list of books considered by the anonymous Christian author to be scriptural. It was made probably at the end of the 2nd century, probably in the west, maybe in Rome.

The author of the Muratorian Canon accepts many of the books that came to be included in the New Testament—22 of the books—but he doesn't accept the Book of Hebrews, James, First and Second Peter, or Third John. He accepts 22 of the 27. He also, though, accepts the Apocalypse of Peter as part of the canon, and he accepts a book called The Wisdom of Solomon as part of the canon. He rejects certain books. For example, there was a book in the 2nd century that was very popular called The Shepherd, written by a guy named Hermas that almost made it into the New Testament—it's included in some canon lists. The anonymous author of the Muratorian Canon says, The Shepherd is not to be accepted because it was written by a guy name Hermas in recent times. It doesn't go back to apostolic times, so this author doesn't think that The Shepherd of Hermas can be included as scripture, even though other Christians were seeing it as a scriptural book.

Throughout the 2nd, and 3rd, and into the 4th century, different Christians argued for the canonicity of a variety books based on four major criteria. There were four criteria that were used. First, a book had to be ancient to be accepted into the canon. It couldn't be something written recently. That's why The Shepherd of Hermas comes to be excluded, because it doesn't go back near to the time of Jesus. Second, a book had to be apostolic, meaning it had to be written by an apostle or by a companion of the apostles. The Gospels of the New Testament don't claim to be written by apostles, but that's why they're given apostolic names—Matthew, Mark, Luke, and John—because to be included in the canon, they have to be apostolic. So even though they're anonymous, they're given apostolic titles. A book had to be ancient; it had to be apostolic. That's why the letters of Paul get included, for example; that's why Revelation ends up being included; that's why Hebrews ends up being included—because they came to be thought to be written by apostles. Third, a book had to be used widely throughout the Church; it had to have universal usage throughout the Church. It couldn't be just a book used in one little church here or there; it had to be widely used. Fourth, most importantly, a book had to be seen as orthodox. It had to be, in other words, teaching the right teachings and not teaching the wrong teachings—that's why the Gospel of Peter ends up being excluded, because some people thought that it contained a docetic Christology.

When did the canon get finalized? When did Christians finally agree on which books to include? To the surprise of many people today—my students have a real hard time with this one—the first Christian of record to maintain that the New Testament was to consist of the 27 books that we have, and only these 27 books, was the Bishop of Alexandria named Athanasius. Athanasius was a very powerful and important figure in early Christianity. In the year 367, he wrote a letter to his churches in Egypt giving them some pastoral advice, and among them, he listed the books that should be read in the church services. The list that Athanasius provides in the year 367 consists of our 27 books and only our 27 books. This is the first recorded time in Christian history that anybody specified our 27 books as the books of the New Testament. This is some 300 years after the books were written. And even in Athanasius's day, there continued to be disputes. His letter didn't solve the matte, didn't finalize the matter. It wasn't really until about the 5th century that Christians around the world pretty much agreed on the 27 books that we have. There was never an ecumenical church council that made the final decision until the Roman Catholic Church, finally, had a council that decided the issue in the mid-16th century at the Council of Trent. That was the first time that any church council came up with a ratification of the 27 books of the New Testament. That's in the 16th century.

There was never an ecumenical council in the early church that decided the matter; instead, it was based on popular opinion, which of course affected which books would be copied over time. Churches and individuals who were most interested in having copies of the scripture, therefore, produced these 27 books, and they produced some of them more often than others. The Gospel of Mark, for example, was not copied nearly as often as the Gospel of John, but the only books, virtually, throughout the Middle Ages that were being copied were the ones that everybody agreed should be scripture. Other books disappeared from the scene not because there were massive book burnings, but simply because nobody bothered to copy these other books because they weren't accepted as canonical. The surviving copies, then, were lost, or worn out, or destroyed, or simply thrown away. With the invention of the printing press, there was no longer any question about which books would be included in the New Testament, because now, with the printing press, the same 27 books could be printed in the same sequence, time after time, after time, until today. These are the only 27 books in our New Testament.

And so we have the Christian scriptures—the New Testament—the collection of books that has proved more significant for the history and culture of Western Civilization than any other collection of books, without rival in the West for its social and religious importance.

Timeline

63 B.C.	Conquest of Palestine by the Romans.
44 B.C.	Assassination of Julius Caesar.
40 B.C.–4 B.C.	Herod, king of the Jews.
27 B.C.–A.D. 14	Octavian Caesar Augustus as emperor.
4 B.C.?	Jesus' birth.
A.D. 14–37	Emperor Tiberius.
A.D. 26–36	Pilate as governor of Judea.
A.D. 30?	Jesus' death.
A.D. 33?	Conversion of Paul.
A.D. 37–41	Emperor Caligula.
A.D. 41–54	Emperor Claudius.
A.D. 54–68	Emperor Nero.
A.D. 50–60?	Pauline Epistles.
A.D. 65?	Gospel of Mark.
A.D. 66–70	Jewish Revolt and destruction of the Temple.
A.D. 69–79	Emperor Vaspasian.
A.D. 79–81	Emperor Titus.
A.D. 80–85?	Gospels of Matthew and Luke, book of Acts.
A.D. 80–100?	Deutero-Pauline Epistles, 1 Peter, Hebrews, James.
A.D. 81–96	Emperor Domitian.
A.D. 85–105?	Pastoral Epistles.
A.D. 90–95?	Gospel of John.

A.D. 95? .... Book of Revelation.

A.D. 98–117 .... Emperor Trajan.

A.D. 120? .... 2 Peter.

A.D. 110–130? .... Gospels of Peter and Thomas.

A.D. 125? .... Infancy Gospel of Thomas.

A.D. 135 .... Letter of Barnabas.

A.D. 160–225 .... Tertullian.

A.D. 296–373 .... Athanasius.

Glossary

apocalypse: A literary genre in which an author, usually pseudonymous, describes symbolic and often bizarre visions that reveal the heavenly mysteries that make sense of earthly realities.

apocalypticism: A worldview held throughout the ancient world by many Jews and Christians that claimed that the present age is controlled by forces of evil, which would be destroyed at the end of time, when God would intervene in history to bring in his kingdom. This event was thought to be imminent.

apostle: From a Greek word meaning "one who is sent." In early Christianity, the term designated special emissaries of the faith who were representatives of Christ.

autograph: The original manuscript of a document, from a Greek word that means "the writing itself."

canon: From a Greek word that literally means "ruler" or "straight edge." The term is used to designate a recognized collection of texts; the New Testament canon is, thus, the collection of books that Christians have traditionally accepted as authoritative.

Christ: See **messiah**.

covenant: An agreement or treaty between two social or political parties. Ancient Jews used the term to refer to the pact God made with the Jewish ancestors to protect and preserve Israel as his chosen people in exchange for their devotion and adherence to his Law.

Deutero-Pauline Epistles: Ephesians, Colossians, and 2 Thessalonians, letters that have a "secondary" (Deutero) standing among the Pauline Epistles because scholars debate whether they were actually written by Paul.

Docetism: The view that Jesus was not a human being but only "appeared" to be; from a Greek word that means "to seem" or "to appear."

Ebionites: A group of second-century adoptionists who maintained Jewish practices and Jewish forms of worship.

gentile: A Jewish term for a non-Jew.

Gnosticism: A group of ancient religions, closely related to Christianity, that maintained that sparks of a divine being had become entrapped in the present, evil world and could escape only by acquiring the appropriate secret *gnosis* (Greek for "knowledge") of who they were and how they could escape. This *gnosis* was generally thought to have been brought by an emissary descended from the divine realm.

gospel: Literally, "good news." When used for a book, it refers to an account of the sayings and/or deeds of Jesus.

Greco-Roman world: The lands and culture of the Mediterranean from Alexander the Great through the early Roman Empire (c. 300 B.C. to A.D. 300).

heresy: Any worldview or set of beliefs deemed by those in power to be deviant; from a Greek word that means "choice" (because "heretics" have "chosen" to deviate from the "truth"; see **orthodoxy**).

Manuscript: Any handwritten copy of a text.

marcionites: Followers of Marcion, the second-century Christian scholar and evangelist, later labeled a heretic for his docetic Christology and his belief in two Gods, the harsh legalistic God of the Jews and the merciful loving God of Jesus—views that he claimed to have found in the writings of Paul.

messiah: From a Hebrew word that means "anointed one," which translates into Greek as *Christos* (whence our English word *Christ*). The 1st century saw a variety of expectations of what this future anointed one might look like, some Jews expecting a future warrior king like David; others, a cosmic judge from heaven; others, an authoritative, priestly interpreter of the Law; and others, a powerful prophet from God like Moses.

Muratorian Canon: An 8th-century manuscript, copied probably from a 2nd-century original, that lists the books that its author considered to belong to the New Testament canon. This is probably our earliest surviving canon list.

orthodoxy: Literally, "right opinion"; a term used to designate a worldview or set of beliefs acknowledged to be true by the majority of those in power. For its opposite, see **heresy**.

Passion: From the Greek word for "suffering." The passion is used as a technical term for the traditions of Jesus' last days, including his crucifixion (hence, the *Passion narrative*).

Pastoral Epistles: New Testament letters that Paul allegedly wrote to two pastors, Timothy (1 and 2 Timothy) and Titus, concerning their pastoral duties. Most critical scholars doubt whether Paul actually wrote them.

Proto-orthodox Christianity: A form of Christianity endorsed by some Christians of the 2nd and 3rd centuries (including the apostolic fathers) that promoted doctrines that were later declared "orthodox" by the victorious Christian party in the 4th and later centuries, in opposition to such groups as the Ebionites, the Marcionites, and the Gnostics.

pseudonymity: The practice of writing under a "false name," as is evident in a number of pagan, Jewish, and Christian writings from antiquity.

Roman Empire: All of the lands (including Palestine) that had been conquered by Rome and were ruled, ultimately, by the Roman emperor, starting with Caesar Augustus in 27 B.C. Before Augustus, Rome was a republic, ruled by the Senate.

synoptic Gospels: The Gospels of Matthew, Mark, and Luke, which tell many of the same stories, sometimes in the same words, so that they can be placed side-by-side to be "seen together" (the literal meaning of *synoptic*).

textual criticism: Any discipline that attempts to establish the original wording of a text on the basis of its surviving manuscripts.

Torah: A Hebrew word meaning "guidance," "direction," or more woodenly, "law." It is often used as a technical term either for the Law of God given to Moses or for the first five books of the Hebrew Scriptures, which were sometimes ascribed to Moses: Genesis, Exodus, Leviticus, Numbers, and Deuteronomy.

Undisputed Pauline Epistles: Romans, 1 and 2 Corinthians, Galatians, Philippians, 1 Thessalonians, and Philemon. Scholars are, for the most part, unified in judging that these letters were actually written by Paul. See also **Deutero-Pauline Epistles** and **Pastoral Epistles**.

Biographical Notes

Alexander the Great: Alexander of Macedonia, otherwise known as Alexander the Great, was one of the most influential persons in the history of Western civilization. Born in 356 B.C. to King Philip of Macedonia, he succeeded to the throne at the age of 22 upon the assassination of his father. Alexander was driven by his desire for conquest, and through real military genius and ruthless military policy, he quickly managed to conquer Greece, before moving his armies eastward to overcome Asia Minor, Palestine, and Egypt. His major conquest came over Darius, ruler of the Persian Empire, which extended his territories well into what is modern-day India.

Alexander's real historical significance is found in his use of military conquest to spread a previously unheard-of cultural unity to the lands around the Mediterranean. As a youth, Alexander had studied under the great Greek philosopher Aristotle and became convinced of the superiority of Greek culture. As a military conqueror, he actively encouraged the use of the Greek language and the adoption of Greek culture in the lands he ruled, building cities in the Greek style with gymnasia, theaters, and public baths as his administrative centers. He was particularly influential in spreading Greek ways to the upper-class elites throughout his domain. This process of spreading "Greek" (*hellas*) culture throughout the Mediterranean is called *Hellenization*. It played an enormous role in the history of Western civilization and, of course, for the New Testament, which was rooted in Hellenistic culture and was itself written in Greek.

Athanasius: Athanasius was a highly influential and controversial bishop of Alexandria throughout the middle half of the 4th century. Born around 300 A.D., he was active in the large and powerful Alexandrian church already as a young man, appointed as a deacon to the then-bishop Alexander. He served as secretary to the important Council of Nicea in 325 C.E., which attempted to resolve critical issues concerning the nature of Christ as fully divine, of the same substance as God the father, and co-eternal with the father.

As bishop of Alexandria from 328–375, Athanasius was a staunch defender of this Nicene understanding of Christ and a key player in the development of the orthodox doctrine of the Trinity, in which there were three distinct persons (Father, Son, and Spirit) who were, nonetheless, one God, all of the same substance. This defense created enormous difficulties for Athanasius in the face of powerful opposition, to which he himself reacted with a show of force (even violence). He was sent into exile on several occasions during his bishopric, spending nearly 16 years away from Alexandria while trying to serve as its bishop.

Author of numerous surviving works, Athanasius is of most significance for this course for his role in determining which books should be accepted in his churches as sacred Scripture. In 367 A.D., in his 39th annual "Festal Letter," which like all the others, set the date for the celebration of Easter and included pastoral instruction, he indicated that the 27 books that we now have in the New Testament, and only those 27, should be regarded as canonical. This decree helped define the shape of the canon for all time and helped lead to the declaration of other books, such as the Gnostic Gospels and the like, as heretical.

Barnabas: We are not well informed about the historical Barnabas. He is mentioned both by the apostle Paul (Gal. 2:13; 1 Cor. 9:6) and the book of Acts (Acts 9:27; 11:22–26) as one of Paul's traveling companions, and it appears that he was originally a Hellenistic Jew who converted to faith in Christ and became, like Paul, a traveling missionary who spread the faith. The book of Acts goes so far as to consider him one of the "apostles" (Acts 14:4, 14).

The Epistle of Barnabas discussed in this course is attributed to him, but modern scholars are reasonably sure that he could not have written it. The book appears to have been written some time around 130 or 135 A.D., some 60 years or so after the historical Barnabas would have died. The book was attributed to him, then, by Christians who wanted to advance its authoritative claims as being rooted in the views of one of the most important figures from the early years of Christianity.

Irenaeus: Irenaeus was an important theologian and heresiologist of the late 2nd century. Born probably around 130 A.D., he may have been raised in the city of Smyrna and educated, eventually, at Rome. He ended up in the Christian church of Lyon, Gaul (modern-day France), where he was made bishop around 178 A.D. He died around the year 200 A.D.

Irenaeus is our best patristic source for the Gnostic sects of the 2nd century. His best-known book is a five-volume attack on heresy, which he entitled *Refutation and Overthrow of What Is Falsely Called Gnosis*, frequently called simply *Against Heresies*. In it, he gives considerable detail concerning various heretical groups (not simply Gnostics) and, based on his understanding of Scripture and using a full panoply of rhetorical ploys and stratagems, refutes them one by one. This book was used as a source for many of the later heresiologists, including Tertullian and Epiphanius.

Jesus: We do not know when Jesus was born, but if it was during the reign of King Herod of Israel, as recorded in the Gospels of Matthew and Luke, then it must have been sometime before 4 B.C., the date of Herod's death. Jesus was raised in a Jewish home in the small village of Nazareth in Galilee, the northern part of what is now Israel. As an adult, he engaged in an itinerant preaching ministry in largely rural areas of Galilee; there is no record of him visiting any large cities until his fateful journey to Jerusalem at the end of his life. His message was comparable to that found in the prophets of the Hebrew Bible: The people of Israel must repent or they will be faced with judgment. Jesus, though, gave this message an apocalyptic twist, as did many other religious Jews of his day: The coming judgment would be of cosmic proportions and brought by an emissary from heaven, the Son of Man, who would overthrow the forces of evil and establish God's kingdom on earth. When this happened, there would be a serious reversal of fortunes; those in power now would be destroyed and those who suffered and were oppressed now would be exalted. People needed to prepare for this historical cataclysm by turning back to God and keeping his Law, especially as interpreted by Jesus himself.

Despite Jesus' reputation as a healer and exorcist, he was not viewed favorably by Jewish leaders. At the end of his life, he came to Jerusalem during a Passover feast, caused a disturbance in the Temple, and raised the ire and fears of the ruling party, the Sadducees, who were intent on keeping the peace and avoiding any riots during such tumultuous times. They had Jesus arrested and turned him over to the Roman governor, Pontius Pilate, who ordered him crucified as a troublemaker. Scholars dispute the precise year of his death, but it must have been some time around A.D. 30.

Marcion: Marcion was one of the most infamous "heretics" of the 2nd century. Tradition indicates that he was born and raised in Sinope, on the southern shore of the Black Sea, where as a young man, he acquired considerable wealth as a shipping merchant. His father was allegedly the bishop of the Christian church there, who excommunicated his son for his false teachings. In 139 A.D., Marcion went to Rome, where he spent five years developing his theological views, before presenting them to a specially called council of the church leaders. Rather than accepting Marcion's understanding of the Gospel, however, the church expelled him for false teaching. Marcion then journeyed into Asia Minor, where he proved remarkably successful in converting others to his understanding of the Christian message. "Marcionite" churches were in existence for centuries after his death, around 160 A.D.

Marcion's understanding of the Gospel was rooted in his interpretation of the writings of the apostle Paul, whose differentiation between the "Law" (of the Old Testament) and the "Gospel" (of Christ) Marcion took to an extreme, claiming that the old and new were fundamentally different, so much so that they represented the religions of different Gods. Marcion, in other words, was a *ditheist*, who thought that the Old Testament God—who had created the world, called Israel to be his people, and gave them his Law—was a different god from the God of Jesus, who came into the world in the "appearance" of human flesh (because he was not actually part of the material world of the creator-god) to save people from the just but wrathful God of the Jews. Marcion's views were based on his canon of Scripture—the first canon known to be formally advanced by a Christian—which did not, obviously, contain anything from the Old Testament but comprised a form of the Gospel of Luke and 10 of Paul's letters (all those in the present New Testament except 1 and 2 Timothy and Titus).

Paul the Apostle: Paul was a Hellenistic Jew born and raised outside of Palestine. We do not know when he was born, but it was probably sometime during the first decade A.D. Through his own letters and the encomiastic account found in the book of Acts, we can learn something of his history. He was raised as a strict Pharisaic Jew and prided himself in his scrupulous religiosity. At some point in his early adulthood, he learned of the Christians and their proclamation of the crucified man Jesus as the messiah; incensed by this claim, Paul began a rigorous campaign of persecution against the Christians—only to be converted himself to faith in Jesus through some kind of visionary experience.

Paul then became an ardent proponent of the faith and its best-known missionary. He saw his call as a missionary to the Gentiles and worked in major urban areas in the regions of Asia Minor, Macedonia, and Achaia to establish churches through the conversion of former pagans. A distinctive aspect of his message was that all people, Jew and Gentile, are made right with God through Jesus' death and resurrection and by no other means; the practical payoff was that Gentiles did not need to become Jewish in order to be among the people of the Jewish God—in particular, the men did not need to become circumcised.

We know about Paul principally through the letters that he wrote to his churches when problems had arisen that he wanted to address. There are seven letters in the New Testament that undisputedly come from his hand; six others claim him as an author, but there are reasons to doubt these claims. According to the book of Acts, Paul was eventually arrested for socially disruptive behavior and sent to Rome to face trial. An early tradition outside of the New Testament indicates that Paul was martyred there, in Rome, during the reign of the emperor Nero in A.D. 64.

Tertullian: Tertullian, from Carthage (North Africa), was one of the most influential authors of early Christianity. Much of his life is shrouded in obscurity, but it appears that he was born into a relatively affluent family of pagans, around 160 A.D., and received an extensive training in (pagan) literature and rhetoric. He converted to Christianity some time in his mid-30s and then became an outspoken, even vitriolic, proponent of the Christian faith, writing numerous works defending the faith against its cultured despisers (apologies), scathing criticisms of heretics and their beliefs, and severe tractates concerning Christian morality. At some point in his life, he joined a group of schismatics known to history as the Montanists (named after their founder, Montanus), an ethically rigorous, ascetic group that anticipated the imminent end of the world as we know it.

For this course, Tertullian is most important for his anti-heretical writings. A bitter opponent of both Gnostics and Marcionites, he is one of our best sources of information concerning what these groups, especially the latter, believed. His five-volume attack on Marcion, for example, still survives and is our principal means of access to Marcion's life and teaching.

Bibliography

Aune, David. *The New Testament in Its Literary Environment*. Philadelphia: Westminster, 1987. A superb introduction to the genres of the New Testament writings in relation to other literature in the Greco-Roman world.

Bauer, Walter, *Orthodoxy and Heresy in Earliest Christianity*. Trans. Robert Kraft et al. Philadelphia: Fortress, 1971. One of the most important books of the 20th century on the history of early Christianity. Bauer argues against the classical understanding of orthodoxy and heresy by maintaining that what was later called heresy was, in many regions of early Christendom, the oldest and largest form of Christian belief.

Beker, J. Christiaan. *The Heirs of Paul: Paul's Legacy in the New Testament and in the Church Today*. Philadelphia: Fortress, 1991. An engaging study of the Deutero-Pauline and pastoral Epistles, written by one of the leading Pauline scholars of the end of the 20th century.

Brown, Raymond. *An Introduction to the New Testament*. Anchor Bible Research Library. New York: Doubleday, 1997. This is a full and authoritative introduction to all of the major issues pertaining to the study of the New Testament, by one of the premier New Testament scholars of the second half of the 20th century. It includes extensive and up-to-date bibliographies.

Cameron, Ron. *The Other Gospels: Non-Canonical Gospel Texts*. Philadelphia: Westminster, 1982. An important collection of the earliest Gospels that did not make it into the New Testament canon.

Collins, Adela Yarbro. *Crisis and Catharsis: The Power of the Apocalypse*. Philadelphia: Westminster Press, 1984. This is a superb discussion of the authorship, social context, and overarching message of the Revelation of John.

Cross, John Dominic. *Four Other Gospels: Shadows on the Contours of the Canon*. Minneapolis: Winston Press, 1987. An intriguing discussion of four of the major early Christian Gospels that did not make it into the canon of Scripture, including the Gospels of Peter and Thomas.

Ehrman, Bart D. *A Brief Introduction to the New Testament*. New York: Oxford University Press, 2004. An introduction to all the major issues involved in studying the New Testament writings from a historical perspective, written for those coming to the study for the first time.

————. *Lost Christianities: The Battles for Scripture and the Faiths We Never Knew.* New York: Oxford University Press, 2004. A study of the wide-ranging diversity of Christianity in the 2nd and 3rd centuries, of the sacred texts (many of them forged) produced and revered by different Christian groups of the period, and of the struggles that led to the emergence of "orthodox" Christianity prior to the conversion of Constantine. For popular audiences.

————. *Misquoting Jesus: The Story Behind Who Changed the Bible and Why.* San Francisco: HarperSanFrancisco, 2005. A popular treatment of *textual criticism*, the discipline that attempts to reconstruct the "original" writings of the New Testament from the surviving manuscripts.

————. *The New Testament: A Historical Introduction to the Early Christian Writings.* 3rd ed. New York: Oxford University Press, 2004. This volume provides a historically oriented introduction to all of the issues dealt with in this course, by the instructor. It is designed both for use as a college-level textbook and as a resource for anyone interested in the New Testament.

————. *The Orthodox Corruption of Scripture: The Effect of Early Christological Controversies on the Text of the New Testament.* New York: Oxford University Press, 1993. This is a study of the ways scribes were influenced by doctrinal disputes in the early church and of how they modified their texts of the New Testament in order to make them conform more closely with their own theological views. It is best suited for more advanced students.

Elliott, J. K. *The Apocryphal New Testament: A Collection of Apocryphal Christian Literature in an English Translation.* Oxford: Clarendon Press, 1993. An excellent one-volume collection of non-canonical Gospels, Acts, Epistles, and Apocalypses, in a readable English translation with nice, brief introductions.

Froehlich, Karlfried. *Biblical Interpretation in the Early Church.* Philadelphia: Fortress, 1984. A useful discussion of the methods of interpretation prevalent in early Christianity, especially in view of their roots in other interpretive practices of the ancient world.

Gamble, Harry. *The New Testament Canon: Its Making and Meaning.* Philadelphia: Fortress, 1985. This is a clearly written and informative overview of the formation of the canon that shows how, why, and when Christians chose the present 27 books to include in their sacred Scriptures of the New Testament.

Grant, Robert M., and David Tracy. *A Short History of the Interpretation of the Bible*. Philadelphia: Fortress, 1983. A survey of the methods used to interpret the Bible from the earliest of times onward.

Hawthorne, Gerald, and Ralph Martin. *Dictionary of Paul and His Letters*. Downers Grove, IL: Intervarsity, 1993. A "Bible dictionary" with in-depth articles on a wide range of topics pertaining to Paul and his letters, written by prominent evangelical Christians.

Keck, Leander. *Paul and His Letters*. Philadelphia: Fortress, 1979. This is an insightful overview of Paul's theology, as expressed in his letters. It makes for an excellent resource for those who are new to the field.

Kysar, Robert. *John, the Maverick Gospel*. Atlanta: John Knox, 1996. This is one of the best introductions to the distinctive features of John's Gospel, which pays particular attention to how John differs from the synoptics in many of its major perspectives on Jesus.

Metzger, Bruce M., and Bart D. Ehrman. *The Text of the New Testament: Its Transmission, Corruption, and Restoration*. 4th ed. New York: Oxford, 2005. This is the classic introduction to the history, data, and methods of New Testament textual criticism, in a newly revised edition. Portions of the book require a basic knowledge of Greek, but all English readers can use the book as a tremendous resource.

Nickle, Keith. *The Synoptic Gospels: Conflict and Consensus*. Atlanta: John Knox, 1980. One of the best introductory discussions of the background and message of the three synoptic Gospels.

Parker, David. *The Living Text of the Gospels*. Cambridge: Cambridge University Press, 1997. This is perhaps the best introduction to New Testament textual criticism for beginners, in which the author argues that the modifications made by the Christian scribes who copied the text show that they did not see it as a dead object but as a living tradition.

Pilch, J. *What Are They Saying about the Book of Revelation?* New York: Paulist Press, 1978. This is a clear and useful overview of the perspectives on the Book of Revelation found among modern scholars.

Roetzel, Calvin. *The Letters of Paul: Conversations in Context*. 3rd ed. Atlanta: John Knox, 1991. This is perhaps the best available introductory discussion of the Pauline Epistles, which includes an examination of the issues of authorship and date, as well as a sketch of the major themes of each letter.

Rowland, Christopher. *The Open Heaven: A Study of Apocalyptic in Judaism and Early Christianity*. New York: Crossroad, 1982. A major overview of early Jewish and Christian apocalypticism, as evidenced in the surviving texts.

Wedderburn, A. J. M. *The Reasons for Romans*. Edinburgh: T & T Clark, 1988. The most complete book-length discussion of the reasons that Paul wrote his letter to the Romans: to explain his gospel of salvation apart from the Law to the predominantly Gentile Roman Christians, in light both of the tensions between Jews and Gentiles there and of his own impending journey to Jerusalem.

Notes

Notes

Notes